Keith,

I wish you great
success as you lead
Polythrop on this important
journey!

Feb. 08

ADVANCE ACCLAIM

ADVANCE ACCLAIM

ADVANCE ACCLAIM

Faisal Hoque
Terry A. Kirkpatrick

Sustained Innovation
Converging Business
and Technology to
Achieve Enduring
Performance

BTm
Press

Library of Congress Control Number: 2006940715

Sustained innovation: converging business and technology to achieve enduring performance/Faisal Hoque and Terry A. Kirkpatrick. p.cm.

Includes index.

ISBN   0-9788175-0-8
        978-0-9788175-0-3

1. Managerial economics. 2. Industrial management. 3. Information technology— Management. 4. Business Strategy 5. Business Management. I. Faisal Hoque and Terry Kirkpatrick.

Editor-at-Large: Diana L. Mirakaj
Design and Composition: Lorenzo Ottaviani

©2007 by the BTM Press
An Imprint of
Business Technology Management Corporation (BTM Corporation)

The publisher offers discounts on this book when ordered in quantity for bulk purchases or special sales. For more information, contact: BTM Press, 2777 Summer Street, Suite 702, Stamford, CT 06905. Website: www.btmpress.com; E-mail: sales@btmcorporation.com.

Printed in the United States of America.

First Printing, February 2007

ISBN   0-9788175-0-8
        978-0-9788175-0-3

For my family, friends and colleagues

—Faisal Hoque

For Jeri, Sara, Rachel and Jeremy

—Terry A. Kirkpatrick

"Your living is determined not so much by what life brings to you as by the attitude you bring to life; not so much by what happens to you as by the way your mind looks at what happens."

—*Kahlil Gibran*

"The future has become the present, and every dream—except those dreams that involve preconceived ideas—will have a chance to be heard. Anything of importance will remain; anything useless will disappear. However, it is not our responsibility to judge the dreams of others."

—*Paulo Coelho*

Contents

Acknowledgements

This book would not have been possible without the active contribution of Diana Mirakaj and Lorenzo Ottaviani at every step. We especially thank our other colleagues at the BTM Corporation, particularly the dedicated members of the research, products, and services teams, for their creation and application of Business Technology Management (BTM) in the real world settings where innovation takes life.

We are equally indebted to all of those in industry and academia who since 1999 have joined with us to study and advance our thinking on Business Technology Management. Their insights played a major role in our three previous books, on which this volume builds. In particular, Dr. V. Sambamurthy and Dr. Robert Zmud, Co-chairs of the BTM Institute's Academic Council, always provide outstanding research leadership.

For their review of the book and enthusiastic support, we are grateful to Professor Muhammad Yunus, Sir Paul Judge, Dr. Leslie Willcocks, Professor Prabhu Guptara, Sujeet Kumar, Alan Ganek, and Dr. Ritu Agarwal.

—*Faisal Hoque and Terry A. Kirkpatrick*

Convergence: The Key to Knowledge-based Innovation

Who really invented the steam engine?
What Peter Drucker thought about innovation.
Converging disciplines and innovation.
Innovation as a process.

You cannot begin to think of innovation as a process without studying Peter Drucker, the "father of modern management," and his thoughts on systematic innovation, entrepreneurship, organizational structure, knowledge workers (a term he coined a decade ago), and community.

In this book we explore knowledge-based, technology-enabled innovation that is driven by the convergence of business and technology. To illustrate this and stimulate your thinking we tell stories from around the world about large corporations, government, education, medicine and social enterprises. Innovation has common characteristics across all of these fields.

But first it is important to highlight how our thinking has been deeply influenced and shaped by "the most enduring management thinker of our time"—Peter Drucker. He, of course, was as concerned with non-profit enterprises as he was the for-profits. His concept of the convergence of multi-disciplinary fields of knowledge inspired us to take a new look at the role of business technology convergence in sustained innovation.

Drucker's book, *Innovation & Entrepreneurship* (Collins, May 26, 1993), remains in our opinion the definitive work on business innovation. In it, Drucker succinctly writes: "Systematic innovation therefore consists in the purposeful and organized search for changes, and in the systematic analysis of the opportunities such as changes might offer for economic or social innovation."

He outlines seven sources for innovative opportunities that should be monitored by those interested in starting an entrepreneurial venture.

1. *The Unexpected*—the unexpected success, the unexpected failure, the unexpected outside event;
2. *The Incongruity*—between reality as it actually is and reality as it is assumed to be or as it "ought to be;"
3. *Innovation based on a process need;*
4. *Changes in industry or market structure that catch everyone unaware;*
5. *Demographics* (population changes);
6. *Changes in perception, mood and meaning;*
7. *New knowledge,* both scientific and nonscientific.

He goes on to explain each of these seven sources in great detail with practical examples. In particular, he outlines "New Knowledge" or knowledge-based innovation:

> *"Knowledge-based innovation is the "super-star" of entrepreneurship. And like most super-stars, knowledge-based innovation is temperamental, capricious, and hard to manage. Not to mention it has the longest lead-time of all innovations. One other key characteristic of knowledge-based innovations—and a truly unique one—is that they are almost never based on one factor but on the convergence of different kinds of knowledge, not all of them scientific and technological."*

It is this viewpoint that drove much of our critical thinking about the convergence of business and technology management, and innovation driven by systematic processes. Drucker illustrates innovation from cross-disciplinary knowledge with many real life examples. He uses the development of the steam engine to make several points about innovation.

One is that innovation is usually not the result of a mad scientist's eureka moment. James Watt, who usually gets credit for the steam engine, was preceded by Thomas Newcomen whose invention in 1712 was used to pump water out of a coal mine. "Both men," Drucker writes, "were organized, systematic, purposeful innovators."

Second, innovations often are the result of many people approaching a challenge with different ideas and knowledge. Watt brought to Newcomen's engine the knowledge of how to ream a smooth cylinder and the design for a condenser.

Third, innovations often unfold over time. The refinements to Newcomen's work by Watt and others occurred over many decades.

The airplane, Drucker points out, could have only come about from the convergence of two types of knowledge—the gasoline engine and the mathematics of aerodynamics. The knowledge required for innovation is not always technical. The development of the modern newspaper, for example, depended not only on the telegraph and the teletype, but also on mass literacy and mass advertising. The modern bank, ala J.P. Morgan and others, depended on the convergence of basic consumer banking and venture capitalism.

Peter Drucker spoke of knowledge-based innovation in 1985. He identified the convergence of different disciplines and points of view as the petri dish for innovation. What he didn't discuss then, because it was still early, was the huge role that "business technology" would come to play in innovation. Since his time technology (more specifically information technology) has so permeated our organizations as to be indispensable. At many companies, it accounts for more than half of capital spending. Simply put, innovation today requires the convergence of the management of business and the management of technology. Effective management of business technology can not only create more profits for mega corporations but can also forever alter social enterprises that serve the "bottom of the pyramid"—the underdeveloped and the underprivileged. Let us look at a couple of examples:

A man on a bright red motorcycle roars through the stilted houses of rural O Siengle, Cambodia, and slows as he passes the elementary school. At this moment, a WiFi chip in a box strapped to the cycle shoots email wirelessly to a solar-powered computer in the school, and receives outgoing email in return. Later, the driver and four others rendezvous at another school with a satellite uplink to send the email on its way. The 800 villagers of O Siengle, who have no electric or telephone lines, are connected to the globe. This project was the work of two former MIT Media Lab students who created a company called First Mile Solutions to provide asynchronous Internet connections in remote areas.

A company called Drishtee ("vision" in Hindi) contracts with a state government to provide services to remote villages—land records, driver's licenses, and complaints about government services. A WiFi-enabled bus passes village kiosks and communications between government and villagers are asynchronously exchanged. Local entrepreneurs run the kiosks, taking 80 percent of the profits. The cost to the villagers is far lower than if they had to give up a day or more to travel to the state offices.

The real innovation is not technological. It is in the business model, a partnership of government, Drishtee and local kiosk operators. Moreover, their innovation was the insight that real time connectivity was too expensive for the villagers and not even necessary to meet their needs. These people don't even need telephones. "Who would I call?" one asked. No one he knew had a phone.

Superimposing a massive telecommunications infrastructure on these rural areas—a "If we build it, you will use it" strategy—would have been folly. The potential customers could not have afforded it. Think of this when you see companies spend hundreds of millions on computer systems that give end users far more than they need, or that are far too complicated for them to adapt to, or that do not let them do what they need to do.

Unfortunately, our ability to manage business technology has not kept pace with our creation of it. In many organizations we still have two camps—technophiles and technophobes—and if they aren't at war, they are wary of each other. In too many organizations the "business side" comes up with a plan and throws it over the wall to the "technology side" to implement. Because technology is so embedded in the way things work today, they should have been sitting and planning together from the very beginning.

But for the first 50 years of the computer age we had no standardized way of doing this. We depended on creative but ad hoc decisions about business technology. Technology executives would create a plan, and if it worked, fine; if it didn't they moved on.

Innovation isn't haphazard. Its core is a creative idea, of course, but it only becomes effective when part of a process: a leader recognizes a need, assembles an organization and designs processes to meet it, and then applies business technology to make it work. It is not the invention of a new technology that matters so much as it is its application—understanding its role when developing a strategy or designing an organization or its processes. That is why we call it "business technology," to underscore the fact that information technology is of value only when it advances the organization's "business."

To create an environment where technology helps shape (rather than simply enable) strategic choices, leading enterprises are working to synchronize (rather than simply align) their business and technology decision-making. And in the best-managed modern enterprises, technology will converge with the business as completely as, say, sound financial management.

Increasingly, this will be the source of all competitive successes. It is a cross-disciplinary management practice that allows professionals to innovate sustainable business models.

Sustained innovation requires a seamless, structured management approach that begins with board and CEO-level issues and connects all the way through technology investment and implementation. Effective Business Technology Management (BTM) offers this, and it has the potential to forever change how corporations, governments, education, NGOs, and social enterprises think of technology's strategic use for socio-economic development, which will in turn have a profound effect on the human condition. This is the message of this book.

It was not until the mid-twentieth century, with the publication of Drucker's *Concept of the Corporation* (1946) and *Practice of Management* (1954), that management became a discipline accessible to managers all over the world. Until then each student or practitioner of management focused on separate areas, some on organization, some on people, and so on. His books codified management, organized it, and systematized it. Within a few years, management became a worldwide force. However it did not bring together business and technology management. It couldn't have, as the advancement of technology did not drive business innovation in the way it does today. This is the role of BTM—a systematic approach to creating sustained innovation.

Our research for a cross-disciplinary management practice to converge business and technology began in 1999. After several years of extensive and collaborative research and development, we published *The Alignment Effect: How to Get Real Business Value Out of Technology* (2002), which defined the emerging concepts of BTM.

Continuing our research agenda, we then published *Winning The 3-Legged Race: When Business and Technology Run Together* (2005). It shows that it is possible to subject business technology to a comprehensive set of management standards. Furthermore, this book highlights that this is not just a technology issue. It is, instead, a business issue, and it will not see resolution until enterprises have a fundamentally better way to manage technology's contribution to the value chain.

In our next publication, *Six Billion Minds: Managing Outsourcing in the Global Knowledge Economy* (2006), we looked into the management challenges and innovation opportunities in light of the profound impact of globalization and the emergence of the knowledge economy.

Using case studies from large companies, social enterprises, and the government sector, *Sustained Innovation: Converging Business and Technology to Achieve Enduring Performance* shows how enterprises can innovate to survive and even thrive in the knowledge-based global economy. Our search for innovation has taken us from the doorsteps of American corporate giants to the home of the Nobel Peace Prize in Oslo, Norway, from the R&D

centers of Israel to India's new economy, from the enterprising government of Algeria to the inspiring operations of Grameen in remote villages of Bangladesh. It is a story of global innovation today, but, furthermore, it is the story of human potential. We hope you will enjoy reading this book as much as we have enjoyed writing it.

Why Innovation?
Why Now?

An introduction to innovation. The SpinBrush and the Village Phone. A model for thinking about innovation. What will Steve Jobs do now? The death of friction and the birth of commodity hell. It's the people, stupid. Who is breathing down your neck?

I f you've ever paused in a drugstore to play with a Crest SpinBrush toothbrush—you can try it out by pushing a button through the plastic package, as its designers want you to do—you came in touch with innovation, 21st Century style.

This little gadget broke all the rules on the way to becoming the nation's best-selling toothbrush, manual or electric, helping Crest to regain its spot as the number one oral care brand and giving Procter & Gamble its 12th billion-dollar brand.

And it is an excellent illustration of profitable innovation: it started as an invention, an innovative application of existing technology, but for it to become a powerhouse product P&G had to be innovative in how it built a business around it. P&G had to reach outside of its corporate walls, create a new kind of partnership, bend and break its go-to-market protocols, and create new business processes — in effect, create a new business model.

None of this happened by accident. The original idea for SpinBrush was a light bulb over the head event—it came to "serial inventor" John Osher in the aisle of a Wal-Mart store—but connecting with that idea and turning it into a profitable product was the result of a management strategy and process. Here's the real secret of sustained innovation: it requires a business process that links the right people with the right ideas in a way that advances the firm's strategy.

Now let's go halfway around the world to the village of Khorsuti in Bangladesh for a different look at innovation.

In my [Faisal Hoque's] native Bangladesh, 97 percent of homes and virtually all rural villages lack a telephone, making the country one of the least wired in the world. This has blocked development and contributed to the continued impoverishment of individual Bangladeshis.

To address this, Grameen (the Bengali word for "village") Bank, a micro-finance institution, formed two entities: Grameen Telecommunications, a non-profit organization to provide phone services in rural areas, and Grameen Phone Ltd., a joint venture of Grameen Telecommunications and Norway's Telenor. It has become Bangladesh's dominant mobile carrier. Grameen Phone helps local entrepreneurs, usually women, set up village phones, selling services to residents at a reasonable price. The company and the entrepreneurs profit, and the villagers get affordable connectivity.

My father grew up in the village of Khorsuti in the Faridpur district, which didn't have electricity until six years ago. He went to engineering school and became one of the national government's most senior civil engineers, dealing with water resource management. Retired now, he visits Khorsuti often, and when he's there I can talk to him, wherever I am in the world, thanks to innovations of Telenor and Grameen.

Telenor is the majority owner of Grameen Phone. I met with its CEO and President, Jon Fredrik Baksaas, in Oslo just before the Nobel Prize ceremonies in the fall of 2005. Baksaas shared that, despite Grameen's altruistic aims, Bangladesh is one of his company's fastest growing markets and has one of its highest gross profit margins.

This is the meaning of "the global knowledge economy"—technology innovation in Norway and business innovation in Bangladesh.

Innovation occurs when people, skills, organizations and technology are mixed and matched in unusual and productive ways.

Let's step back from these positive stories to the turbulent economic environment that is propelling innovation to the forefront.

If you are trying to lead an organization today, or you're just an employee hoping to hang on to your job, you know that this economy makes the '80s and '90s look positively tranquil.

When we try to articulate what is happening to us in this new era, we resort to a familiar set of words: globalization, outsourcing, offshoring, information age, innovation, age of connectivity, disaggregated corporation, death of command and control, real time corporation, knowledge economy, sustainability.

As with a dozen blind men touching an elephant and describing what they feel, each of these terms is relevant as far as it goes, but each addresses only part of the whole. To choose one as a lens through which to view life and business in the 21st Century is to run the risk of missing the larger picture.

As a first step in organizing our thinking about these forces, and designing a response, we can group these terms in two categories. Information, knowledge and innovation might be considered the "what." Connectivity, disaggregation and partnerships might be considered the "how."

In other words, what companies need today to survive is information, which can be analyzed and turned into knowledge, which can then point them to innovation. We get there by connecting, disaggregating and reaching out in new ways.

Why Innovation? Why Now?

If there is nothing new about innovation—think printing press, cotton gin, telephone, light bulb, etc.—why has it captured the imagination of every CEO, magazine editor and conference planner today?

Why do successful companies like GE, IBM and P&G proclaim it from their rooftops?

TASK

As you read this book, as you observe your company (you do observe your own company, don't you?), and as you read about other companies, look for these forces lurking behind otherwise inexplicable actions.

We'll have much to say about the nature of innovation throughout the book. For now let's look into some of the big forces behind this phenomenon.

The Death of Friction

As any student in Economics 101 who has not slept through the lectures knows, a free market exists only when there are sufficient suppliers to create real competition and when there is price transparency, i.e., the consumer knows who is offering what for what price.

One definition of friction is anything that prevents a free market. This friction can result from distance: if the nearest competitors are too far away to be practical for the buyer, the local seller has an upper hand. Today Amazon, just to name one example, has "set up shop" in every town, competing with the local storefronts.

Friction results from incomplete knowledge. Today websites galore create price transparency for just about anything; you can compare products and prices online, and you don't have to pay top dollar for a second-rate product out of ignorance anymore. What does this do to businesses offering second-rate products at higher prices? How will they adjust when their cover of friction is blown?

QUESTION

If commodities are necessary, and people will pay for them, is there any business model for offering them that will be profitable long-term?

Many, many businesses have ridden on the back of friction for so long they become disoriented when it evaporates. This is what we might call "macro" friction; it exists in the marketplace.

Another kind of friction is "micro," i.e., it exists within the firm. (This is how economists might label it. We won't push economists on you often in this book, but at least they have words for these things.) Using technology, and redesigning their business processes, Dell and Wal-Mart eliminated much of the friction in the chain all the way from suppliers to customers. And their competitors were blindsided. What will they do?

Commodity Hell

Barriers to entry into many industries have fallen. It's not easy to start up a railroad, but you can start a personal computer company by outsourcing just about everything to other companies with specialties in design or manufacturing. And so IBM, an innovator of personal computers, abandons the business as PCs become commodities. And Dell, with a superior PC business model, offers a commodity PC for $300, while at the same time rebranding its top of the line boxes under the "XPS" label and offering special features and services—an effort to stay a step ahead of commoditization.

Unpredictable Competitors

Apple launches the innovative iPod and iTunes—an innovation in product and business model. Although there are similar products on the market, Apple captures the world's imagination with superior design and a unique store for music, one that sidesteps potential opposition from music companies trying to protect their rights.

Meantime, cell phone companies start offering phones that can download and play music, counting on the huge installed base of cell phones and the instant gratification of being able to download music wherever you are. In the first quarter of 2006, Sony Ericsson's profits more than tripled due to sales of its Walkman-branded music phones. Who would have thought cell phones could double as music players? What will Apple's Steve Jobs do?

This book is primarily about large organizations, but the forces at work on these organizations today, the forces that drive them to innovate, can be seen in more familiar settings.

What can we learn, for example, from a camera shop and an art print dealer?

Both do business in the small town where I [Terry Kirkpatrick] live. I would drop into the camera shop when I was in the market for a camera, chat with a knowledgeable clerk and look over several of the latest models. The only alternative would have been to drive 45 minutes to a bigger store, where there were more models to look at but less of a personal relationship to be had. Not long ago I went into this camera shop and discovered that it had very few cameras left to sell. Now it seemed to be concentrating on picture frames and other products.

What happened? Was it the big box stores? Or, more likely, was it the fact that I can go online in my family room, order a camera and have it delivered to my door in a few days? The camera shop was a victim of the death of friction.

The print dealer sold antique posters and art prints from a little storefront shop, catering to repeat clients and casual window shoppers. I met him one day at a backyard barbeque, where I learned of his business.

"Why don't you put your business on the Web?" I asked him.

"What's that?" he asked.

Six months later he invited me to his home. There on his PC he showed me how he now had clients all around the world who found him on the Web and were buying from him. His innovation was not technical—the PC and the Web weren't new. (He hired a teenager he knew to build his website.) His innovation was his business model. He in effect made the entire world his market. He seized on the death of friction to grow. And he no doubt became an unpredictable competitor to unknown art dealers around the world.

And whether you realize it or not, you are a player in this new global, knowledge, information age, digitized economy. You can still have a garage sale to get rid of that junk in your basement, or you can stay in your pajamas and put it up for sale to the world on e-Bay.

QUESTION

If you were in the digital camera business, do you think you might want to pay a little attention to the cell phones with built-in cameras?

The only response to these huge forces is to do something different, and that's why innovation is Topic A today. Perhaps you can incorporate technology into a new version of your product (but so can your competitors). Perhaps you can change your business processes to reduce cost, increase speed and respond more intelligently to your customers (but so can your competitors). Perhaps you should consider changing your business model—find new customers or new ways to please existing customers. So can your competitors, so you'll just have to be faster and smarter at it. This is most likely your best chance to create competitive advantage.

"We've prepared GE to innovate by making it central to our business process. Our leaders know we have to innovate."

—Jeffrey Immelt
Chairman and CEO, GE

It's the People, Stupid

As a second step in understanding what is happening to our organizations, let's add another word to the pile: people. If you as a leader focus on people, all of these other things—globalization, outsourcing, disaggregation, and the like—will fall into place.

There are four groups of people that matter: those who work within your organization, those on the outside with whom you set up formal partnerships, those on the outside with whom you form ad hoc learning relationships, and those you aim to please with a product or service.

Innovation is born in the minds of people who have the raw materials of information and knowledge. Apple, for instance, got the iPod idea from someone on the outside—Steve Fadell, a technology innovator who was shopping the idea around when Apple jumped on it. The leader's task is connecting and managing these people so that innovation can surface and be put to use.

Consider, as an example, Procter & Gamble's approach to employees, customers and outside partners. It provides its employees around the world with the latest communications and idea-sharing technology; for example, on its intranet site is an "Ask Me" feature through which anyone can pose a question to the company's 10,000 technical people.

Despite its world class R&D department, P&G reaches out in various ways to scientists and engineers beyond its walls for ad hoc solutions to problems. And on its website, it invites anyone, but particularly its customers, to send in ideas and get involved in the company's innovations: "Do you have the next product, package, or technology that will help improve consumers' lives? P&G is actively seeking opportunities to connect with innovators from around the world."

Indeed, CEO Alan G. Lafley has decreed that half of all of the company's innovations should come from the outside. So while it is looking for technical product innovations, it is doing so through a new way of conducting business—connecting new people in new ways.

Making It Work

Now let's add the last, and most important, element of this model for sustained innovation. The connections among these key groups of people are enabled by technology. The information these people have is processed by technology. Their knowledge is held by and accessed through technology. The modern corporation could not operate without technology, and companies apparently understand its critical role, because they are pouring half of all their capital investment into it.

It follows that it is essential for them to manage this technology well. Ah, if it were only so.

> "The Internet has been a major advance for us here. If I've got a problem I've got to solve, or if I have an idea in an area, I can be in touch with someone somewhere around the globe within 24 to 48 hours who has the answer or idea that I need. Neither of us knew each other beforehand. It allows you to exploit the entrepreneurial spirit and the tremendous intellectual capability that exists outside the company."
>
> —*Gilbert Cloyd*
> *CTO, P&G*

The evidence is that corporations and other organizations are wasting millions of dollars on technology. At least half of all information technology projects fail. Half of all outsourcing deals eventually fall apart. The dollars lost in these efforts can be added up. What is impossible to measure is the lost opportunity. It's one thing to say that the FBI has thrown away millions of dollars trying to digitize its records and connect its agents by email. It's quite another to wonder how this has affected the bureau's ability to identify potential terrorists.

Are your current technology projects on budget and on time?

This is a systemic malaise, by which we mean that it's not necessarily the fault of any individual executive or organization. We simply haven't—all of us—adopted management disciplines that align the business and technology sides of our organizations. Part of the reason is that the computer age is still relatively young, and it has changed constantly, and we've been reacting to the rapid fire of events instead of managing them. Another reason is that the business and technology sides of the organization haven't fully understood each other and developed a trust in each other.

But at some point technology crossed the line between being just a tool and being a strategic element in the business. That meant that the business could no longer be managed without simultaneously managing the technology it runs on, with the same people looking at both as an integrated whole. Sometimes a business idea dictates, and a technology solution is found. Sometimes a new technology dictates, and business processes—and even new business models—are built around it.

In companies that do it well, their business and technology are said to be "converged." It is not common yet, but it's also not hard to find such companies. Look at those that do well in the marketplace, who consistently beat their competitors, and you're likely to find a sophisticated interaction of business and technology.

The successes we've seen are due to the brilliance and creativity of individual executives. What we have not had in the realm of business technology until recently is a management standard, a framework, a set of guidelines that can lead to repeatable results. The accounting world has this, for example, but accounting as a profession had a head start on information technology of several hundred years.

The innovation model we set forth in this book uses the convergence of business and technology management as the key to the organizational structures, processes, information and technology companies need to generate sustained innovation. This sustained innovation is profitable, advances the company's strategy, and, because it flows through a process, is repeatable.

It begins at the top, with the CEO and the board, where the company's overall strategy is set. Is it to be lean? To be agile? Or both? Is it to protect a position in existing markets or to explore new ones? Each of these broad goals requires a different technology deployment, and the technology must be part of the planning.

It is in such planning, and in the information generated to inform it, that companies can create the unique business model and processes most likely to deliver success.

Think companies have mastered such a strategic use of technology?

In a recent *Harvard Business Review* article, Harvard Professor Robert Kaplan and colleague Andrew Pateman call for a new corporate "office of strategy management." Why? Their research reveals that:

- Two-thirds of IT organizations develop strategic plans that are not linked to the organization's strategy. "This," the authors say in an understatement, "is extraordinary."

- "Most devastating," they say, 95 percent of employees in most organizations do not understand their organization's strategy.

Extraordinary? Devastating? Yes, and in our experience, all too common.

Are your business and technology managed together? What's missing?

The Innovative Mind

Seeing in new ways. Challenging our favorite assumptions.
Why leaders fail. The right mindset in the right environ-
ment. How to think about this stuff called information.
The organization as an information-processing organism.

Back from U.S. Navy service in World War II, a college degree
in hand, as well as rejection letters from all 23 of the medical
schools to which he had applied, young Julius Jacobson enrolled at
the University of Pennsylvania to pursue a Ph.D. degree in cell
physiology. In the lab he stared through a microscope, all day
every day. That daily routine in his career detour would one day
have a profound effect on the practice of medicine.

Eventually accepted by Johns Hopkins and earning his medical
degree, Jacobson did his surgical residency at Presbyterian
Hospital in New York and then took the position of Director of
Surgical Research at the University of Vermont.

His first project there, as part of testing a new veterinary drug,
was to denervate a dog's carotid artery, i.e., stop the nerves from
functioning. He realized that the only way to know if all of the
nerves had been interrupted was to cut the artery in two and then
reconnect it. But he and everyone else in medicine "knew" that
the artery was too small for that.

And then it came to him—look at the artery under a microscope. Aha! The problem was not that the artery was too small to

reconnect. The problem was that it was too small to see. This insight, in 1960, launched the field of microvascular surgery. The re-implantation of severed limbs, heart bypass surgery and a myriad of other surgical procedures became possible. "And the only reason I had that idea was because I couldn't get into medical school and had spent so much time in front of a microscope," Dr. Jacobson says.

"Our success is due, in part, to not just an ability but a willingness to look at things differently."

—Michael Dell
Chairman, Dell

There is one more important piece to this story for us. Dr. Jacobson realized that vascular surgeons needed to have an assistant simultaneously viewing the operating field microscopically. And so he invented the "diploscope," a two-person microscope. Now his intuition, which had become an idea, was transformed into an innovation, meaning that it could be used to create value.

We can learn a great deal about innovation from this story:

- It often results from the cross-fertilization of ideas in different fields.
- To have value, it must find its way into the hands of those who can use it.
- It is the solution to a problem or a need.
- It is often serendipitous.

Most importantly, this story illustrates that very often what we "know" just isn't so. Here's a good example of that. You probably know the famous quote attributed to Thomas Watson, Founder of IBM: "I think there is a world market for maybe five computers." It's a good example of a smart executive "knowing" something that just isn't true. But here's the best lesson in this—

we all "know" Watson said this, but there is no evidence that he ever did! How much untested "knowledge" do we carry around in our heads?

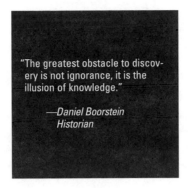

"The greatest obstacle to discovery is not ignorance, it is the illusion of knowledge."

—Daniel Boorstein
Historian

The innovation that will open up the next opportunity for your company probably lies just beyond the boundary of what you and your colleagues think you know.

Equally true, the next big threat to your success probably lies just beyond the boundary of what you think you know.

QUESTION

What do you know or assume about your company, customers, partners, competitors and marketplace? Have you tested those assumptions?

The burden of this book is that, because technology is the engine of business today, organizations can become truly innovative only by converging the management of business and technology. This is because a business model and processes will be involved in wringing any value out of a new product or service, and business models and processes today are built on technology. If they are designed or managed without technology in mind, realizing the value will be more difficult or impossible.

Innovation can also occur in the business model and processes themselves. Without the full integration of business and technology, however, the effort to realize the value of these incremental improvements becomes Herculean.

Let's examine why this is so. When business and technology are not integrated, all sorts of bad things can happen. Software designed to automate an existing business process may only speed up an inefficient or ineffective process that isn't contributing maximum business value. On the other hand, adapting processes to fit the rules embedded in software may eliminate some activity that differentiates the company and gives it an advantage. In either case, the outside world is changing, more rapidly than ever—it sometimes presents a change before a project is implemented. Sometimes end users change their minds. Sometimes they balk at anything new that is imposed on them. Sometimes techies fall in love with new technology for its own sake. Sometimes they are never asked what new technology is available that might improve a business process. Little wonder that half of all information technology projects fail!

Innovation is held prisoner to this environment.

In companies where business and technology management are converged—i.e., integrated from the boardroom to the project team—all this ineffective and risky behavior is mitigated. Converging business and technology management creates new flows of information. Communication between business and technology groups is enhanced and formalized. Strategies are created for them to jointly follow. Knowledge of the assets an organization has and the various initiatives it has underway is generated. In essence, the various parts of an organization start talking to each other, and the conversations are based on facts. The business strategy is supported by appropriate processes, and the processes are enabled by appropriate technology. The organization becomes more intelligent.

In the next chapter, we'll explore in more detail how the management of business and technology can be converged, and how this makes innovation possible, but for now let's consider that the very first step toward convergence is a mental attitude: leaders and their organizations have to accept that there is a new way of managing technology. The old "come up with a business plan and throw it over the wall to IT to make it happen" has long been passé.

Similarly, the first step in becoming innovative is an attitude —accepting that the world really has changed. It's learning to see the world in new ways. You can't reconnect a severed artery? Are

> "Nobody should get in the technology business if they're not prepared to live with, 'Oh, geez, the world is changing.' Of course, the world is changing; embrace it. How do we drive growth, how do we embrace the next trend, how do we be a leading-edge innovator?"
>
> —*Charles DiBona*
> *Analyst, Sanford C. Bernstein*

you looking at it in the same old way? We start here, because everything else we say about managing business and technology for innovation will be for naught without the right mindset.

Changing the way you do business requires imagination. An innovative company is run by, and employs, people who can see something new, an opportunity or a threat, and have the willingness to accept it and the ability to respond to it.

> "In most instances, executive mindset failure happens because senior executives made incorrect assumptions. Few companies spend much time focusing on the underlying assumptions of strategic initiatives."
>
> —*Professor Sydney Finkelstein*
> *Amos Tuck School of Business*
> *Dartmouth*

Sounds simple. But if you doubt that smart, successful leaders and big, thriving corporations can fail to realize what is going on —are unable to sense and respond beyond the familiar—pick up a copy of Sydney Finkelstein's *Why Smart Executives Fail*. For six years the Dartmouth professor studied 51 companies in depth, interviewing 197 executives, about failure. Two of his discoveries are important to us here:

1. Most of the failures occurred during major business passages: creating new ventures, dealing with innovation and change,

managing mergers and acquisitions, and addressing new competitive pressures.

2. The failures were caused by four patterns of behavior: flawed executive mindsets that throw off a company's perception of reality, delusional attitudes that keep this inaccurate reality in place, breakdowns in communications systems developed to handle potentially urgent information, and leadership qualities that keep a company's executives from correcting their course.

This gets personal, doesn't it? We are only going to experience more major business passages, and they are going to come at us more rapidly. And the most important thing we can do in this environment is to have clear minds. This is so obvious that we hesitate to write it, and yet Professor Finkelstein's work and other surveys, along with the front pages of our newspapers, tell us that even our major, most successful companies still manage to foul things up.

Finkelstein cites the example of Rubbermaid, one of the most clever consumer product innovators ever. It cranked out a new product every day—high in quality and also in price. But in the mid-90s, the world changed. As the big box retailers, particularly Wal-Mart, ascended, they picked up huge bargaining power over their suppliers. Rubbermaid's CEO, Wolfgang Schmitt, saw this but stubbornly clung to what had made the company successful. He refused to give in to Wal-Mart's cost-cutting demands, and Wal-Mart responded by giving Rubbermaid's shelf space to other suppliers.

TASK

Identify the three biggest changes in your marketplace over the past two years. How might they put you at risk?

Rubbermaid put all of its eggs in the product innovation basket. Its products were excellent but expensive. Wal-Mart showed that lesser and cheaper products from other companies would do just as well. Moreover, Rubbermaid's production and distribution systems were no match for the avant-garde systems through which Wal-Mart linked up with its suppliers. And Rubbermaid's decentralized organization ran on many disparate information systems. The game had changed, and Rubbermaid was unwilling and unable to play in it.

An Innovation Organization

There are many pieces to the innovation puzzle, and they will come together differently for each organization. The many examples of innovative organizations in this book might inspire you, but it is unlikely that you would want to copy any of them exactly.

Here's why. You know that technology itself is no longer a differentiator—everyone can buy the same technology. How it is deployed and managed is the differentiator. You want it to fit your own unique strategy. In the same way, the practice of benchmarking best practices in non-technology areas may no longer itself be a best practice. Why would you want to do what everyone else is doing with regard to, say, your human resources policies and procedures? Don't you want an incentive system designed to advance your own particular strategy?

And so how you go about building an innovative organization ought to be unique. But for every organization, it will start with the right **mindset**—the unexpected must be expected. Who would have thought that cell phones would become cameras and music

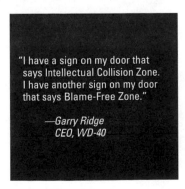

"I have a sign on my door that says Intellectual Collision Zone. I have another sign on my door that says Blame-Free Zone."

—*Garry Ridge*
CEO, WD-40

players? Who would have thought that ordinary, non-techie people would sit down at a personal computer in their homes to configure and order a new personal computer? Or that Dell, which pioneered this online selling model, would decide to open brick and mortar storefronts?

This mindset must start at the top of the organization and permeate every level. The leader must set the example.

Boards of directors have a role in innovation, as well. In our previous book, *Winning the 3-Legged Race*, we described how the boards of some companies have created committees to follow the management of technology. Boards have become managers of risk of the Sarbanes-Oxley variety, but they should also be monitors of strategic risk, i.e., where is the business model vulnerable? What opportunities are we missing? Outside directors can bring different perspectives to the assumptions on which your strategy is based. Perhaps one of them will remember the "microscope" he or she once used in an entirely different endeavor and suggest that things might not be what they appear to be.

Next comes the **environment** in which innovation occurs. This includes the intangibles of culture, i.e., the beliefs, expectations and sense of purpose of those in the organization. Creative thinking and collaboration can be encouraged and rewarded, or in many formal and subtle ways discouraged. It's the leader's job to get it right.

Here's what people might be thinking in a non-innovative environment:

- The last big product launch failed,
  and several people are no longer around.

- Our company is too large to waste time on small ideas.

- We want new ideas, but I'm paid to
  make my numbers on existing business.

- I can't remember manufacturing and
  marketing ever talking about anything.

- We're doing fine; let's let our existing line peak
  before we try something new.

- People are going to get cynical about
  all these change initiatives.

- The last time I made a suggestion, I got my head handed to me.

Of all the changes Lou Gerstner found necessary when he became CEO at IBM, culture was the hardest. He would have preferred to stay away from it and stick with the strategy, analysis and measurement style he had been successful with before. But in *Who Says Elephants Can't Dance* he writes:

> "*I came to see, in my time at IBM, that culture isn't just one aspect of the game—it is the game. In the end, an organization is nothing more than the collective capacity of its people to create value. Vision, strategy, marketing, financial management—any management system, in fact—can set you on the right path and carry you for a while. But no enterprise—whether in business, government, education, health care, or any area of human endeavor—will succeed over the long haul if those elements aren't part of its DNA.*"

The cultural rules that had made IBM so successful had hardened and taken on a life of their own, and when the world changed, they didn't. Although individually smart and capable, Gerstner saw, IBMers were constrained by the culture that had grown up over many years. They couldn't innovate.

QUESTION

Have you empowered your employees to be innovative by providing the organizational structures, processes and technology tools they need to get new ideas into the business?

Culture is not one of those "soft" matters to be dealt with when the "real business" is done. Culture is a complement to the formal, established rules of doing business. An understanding of and commitment to the organization's mission will guide employees when confronted by the unexpected for which no rules exist.

Facing constantly changing threats in Iraq, for example, the U.S. military realized that its old command and control culture doesn't always work fast enough. "We are teaching our soldiers how to think rather than what to think," Lieutenant General R. Steven Whitcomb, Commander of the Third Army, told Professor Michael Useem, Director of the Center for Leadership and Change Management at the Wharton School. On a visit to the Mideast, Professor Useem found parallels for other organizations. "Many companies have moved in the same direction, seeking to become more nimble in their fast-changing and uncertain markets," he wrote. "Sony, for instance, reduced its governing board from 35 directors to nine to facilitate quicker decisions in response to rapidly evolving technologies."

Third is how an organization gathers and processes **information.** Innovation is about information. Imagine for a moment the building you work in stripped of its walls to reveal the plumbing infrastructure—pipes bringing water into the building and distributing it. Imagine now the various uses to which it is put—someone washing his hands with hot water on one floor, someone else using cold on another, a water heater providing hot water, a water fountain cooling it, and so on.

> "Think of a company as an information-processing organism. It gathers data from the market, suppliers, and employees. It makes decisions, implicitly and explicitly. It then communicates and acts on those decisions, with some degree of proficiency."
>
> —*Professor Eric Brynjolfsson*
> *MIT*

Now imagine the building's information infrastructure—telephone and Internet wiring, boxes for incoming and outgoing snail mail, cable television connections, wireless routers, and so on—taking information from the outside or inside and distributing it. Picture the users of this information. An executive studies a computer dashboard of operational data, an employee surfs the Web, an administrative assistant sifts through the paper mail, a committee meets and hears a report, email flows endlessly, operational plans are printed and bound and put on a shelf, and on and on.

New ideas float along in these flows of information. And the leader's task is two-fold: ensure that you have the right flows in place, and create the filters that will capture the valuable ideas. Information can be managed in three ways. One is through organizational structures, such as decision-making groups. Another is in processes, e.g., who hands off what information to whom. The other is automation: technology that gathers and presents data, such as CRM data from a website.

TASK

Identify how your competitors use information for competitive advantage.

In assessing your company as an information organism, look especially at the cross-fertilization of ideas within the four walls. Innovative companies like P&G, W.L. Gore and Google create informal and formal ways for employees in different units and disciplines to work together. When P&G was developing its Crest Whitestrips teeth whitener, it mixed people from its oral care area with people who had developed a new film technology with people from the fabric and home care area who were bleach experts.

Look, too, at the ratio of information coming from the outside to information generated internally. As Bill Joy famously said, "Most of the smart people in the world don't work for you." When Peter Kim took over as Research Chief at Merck & Co. in 2003, he assumed the enormous pressure of feeding the firm's drug pipeline. And the first thing he did was look outside (he himself had come from academia). The company's scientists were terribly insular. In Kim's first three years the company signed an average of 47 partnership deals with other companies. In 1999 it had entered only 10 alliances.

It is vital in the Information Age to view your organization as an information collector, processor and distributor. Equally important is an ability and willingness to see and act upon something new in that information. Seeing opportunity in something new is hard, as Dr. Jacobson found out.

After his discovery of microsurgery, and his creation of a prototype diploscope, Dr. Jacobson began showing the instrument to U.S. corporations. None thought it had much potential as a business. Carl Zeiss, the German optical company, saw something others didn't and helped make the diploscope, and microsurgery, a reality. Today the original instrument resides at the Smithsonian Institution.

In his later years, Jacobson continued to see things in a different way. The monitors in an intensive care ward record a dozen or more vital signs of a patient, but when those squiggly lines move off the screen, the data is lost forever. Remembering too many nights when he was summoned back to the hospital to see what was happening to one of his patients, Jacobson thought: why not capture that vital sign data, and hook up a camera and microphone? That way, a physician, anywhere in the world, could converse with and check the condition of a patient. He considers this project, which he calls "24/7 medicine," the most important in his career.

The technology for this project is nothing new. Microscopes weren't new, either. Then again, innovation has never been just about technology. It has always been about seeing a new way to use it.

An Innovation Model

Xerox fumbles. CEOs can't get no satisfaction. Creating
innovation networks. Looking outward. Reorganizing inside.
New groups, new goals, new attitudes. Xerox recovers.

John Seely Brown, former Chief Scientist at Xerox and Director
of its famously innovative Palo Alto Research Center, describes
the strategy he once used for dealing with company brass as "operational judo." Often when the lab came up with a good idea, for
instance, Brown didn't tell anyone in the company. Instead, he
secretly showed it to customers, got their reaction and made
improvements, and then let the customer present the idea to other
divisions of Xerox. He knew the idea would have greater credibil-
ity coming from a customer.

"We had our own prejudices, too," he says of his scientists. "In
the 1980s, we thought we were the ones who had all the creative
juices that God had meant for mankind to have. We used to think
of marketing people as these poor, brain dead suckers on the East
Coast. It was almost beneath us, unless we were eating lunch, to
spend time with these guys."

PARC is famous, of course, for inventing the Ethernet, the
graphical user interface, the mouse, the laser printer, and one of
the earliest personal computers, the Alto. Xerox is infamous, of

course, for not capitalizing on these inventions and losing them to Apple, 3Com and other companies.

As we build an innovation model in this chapter, we can draw some lessons from the oft-told Xerox/PARC story. One is that an invention is just a curiosity without a business model to take it to market. Xerox didn't have a business model for these inventions, at least not one it put to use, and this has been seen over the years as a major failure.

"Invention without execution is just hallucination."

—*Fred Matteson*
CIO, Fireman's Fund

Perhaps, however, we should cut Xerox management some slack. While it could have gotten into the computer revolution ahead of Apple, 3Com and Microsoft, would that have been in Xerox' strategic interest? Would it have been a distraction amid the company's fierce battles with competitors in its copier business? Would its people have known how to sell computers? Was there even a market for this stuff? Everything must flow from the business strategy, and that means hard decisions about what to pursue and what to leave alone.

When I [Faisal Hoque] was in the Public Sourcing Services group at GE, I learned this lesson. In 1993-94 we developed an innovative business that would allow public sector entities such as municipalities, county governments and school districts to tap into GE's worldwide procurement system, vendor management expertise and buying power. Through a Web interface, these governments could have all the advantages in procurement that they couldn't have operating independently.

It was an innovative business model built on innovative technology. What we didn't realize was that none of these government entities was ready to do business online. In those years it was a novel and untested idea. Other online exchanges bit the dust as well. To the business model and the technology, then, we must add the adoption curve, a key reason customers must be part of innovation. All was not lost: we spread the technology we had created throughout GE to profitable effect. And now we read of Amazon proposing to open up its internal resources—its computing power, for example—to outsiders who will use it to create virtual companies to manufacture and sell physical products. It's a variation on the GE idea, but now perhaps the time is right.

Business strategy must be influenced by new technologies, such as PARC and GE developed. Organizations must have a defined process for monitoring their own technological assets and new technologies being developed elsewhere so that they can examine them for new business opportunities. The opportunities may be disruptive, as with PARC's inventions. Or they may be more incremental—improved data mining and warehousing capabilities, for example, which allow a firm to adapt its strategy toward greater personalization and customer intimacy, a differentiating competitive advantage.

When the management of business and the management of technology are converged, a company can have this two-way conversation—strategy directing activity, and technology discovery informing strategy.

The Xerox/PARC story unfolded two decades ago. Today, in our hyper-competitive environment, a company can't afford to ignore disruptive innovations, such as PARC produced, even if they have a disruptive effect on the company's historic mission. In fact, Xerox has since discovered a model for its promising inventions: it seeds startup companies to exploit them. Burned by criticism of the company's failure to capitalize on its computer discoveries, Xerox Chairman David Kearns in 1988 decided to never lose the advantage again, and he created a corporate venture capital program. From this we can add to our innovation model the necessity for both top-down innovation (as in Kearns' venture capital program) and bottom-up innovation (as in the PARC inventions).

Several other things now come into focus. One is that innovation is not the exclusive preserve of clever scientists hidden away in a skunk works. It must occur everywhere in the organization, in business processes and business models, as well as in products. In fact, a company will likely find more value in business model innovation than in business process innovation, and more value in business process innovation than in product innovation.

> "To be successful today companies have to see their strategy beyond product and beyond the process of producing the product and even beyond the business processes within the company to being able to manage smart business processes in a multinational global network."
>
> —Dr. Kenny Preiss
> Ben Gurion University
> Beer Sheva, Israel

This became clear in a worldwide survey by IBM of 765 CEOs. It revealed that these leaders were focusing almost 30 percent of their innovation efforts on their business models. IBM's financial analysis uncovered an even more interesting bit of information: "Companies that have grown their operating margins faster than their competitors were putting *twice* as much emphasis on business model innovation as under-performers."

Let's draw one more insight from Xerox/PARC. Brown's remarks about the marketers in Xerox are amusing, and the situation within the company sounds very typical. He would later discover, however, when Xerox began launching startups to develop its inventions, that "these guys were bringing as much creativity to the table as we brought." In other words, it takes everyone to make innovation happen, not just the mad scientists.

The point for us is that organizations can no longer tolerate their traditional walls and silos. Remember that innovation is much more than an invention. Deriving any value from a new product requires processes and a business model, and these involve every division and discipline in the organization. The organization has to be designed in such a way as to get everyone talking and working together.

Further, organizations today have to look beyond their boundaries, and that means around the world, if necessary. The days when innovation occurred only in the R&D department are over. The CEOs in IBM's survey said that the top three sources of new ideas were employees, business partners and customers. Internal R&D ranked near the bottom of the list. IBM's analysis again pointed to a payoff: "Companies with higher revenue growth reported using external sources significantly more than slower growers."

If it were only as simple as throwing more money at R&D, life would be easier for everyone. But money alone isn't the answer. The consulting firm Booz Allen Hamilton studied the results of the 1,000 companies with the largest spending on R&D and found that R&D spending levels had no apparent impact on sales growth, gross profit, operating profit, enterprise profit, market capitalization, or total shareholder return. It also found that "when a company is seeking to grow through innovation, it's more important to develop a robust business model and good cross-functional capabilities than to boost the R&D budget. Successful innovation requires an exceptional level of cross-functional cooperation among R&D, marketing, sales, service, and manufacturing."

Internal and external collaboration, enabled by technology, are the keys to sustained innovation.

> "Innovation is not the private property of lone geniuses working apart from the mainstream of the business. In any company of reasonable size, innovation is a social process that requires collaboration and communication for idea generation, selecting those ideas for revenue growth that are to be funded, and shaping those ideas into product prototypes and launching them into the marketplace."
>
> —Ram Charan
>   Management Guru

Putting the Pieces Together

There is little doubt, as IBM's CEO survey and others show, that corporations take innovation seriously, seeing it as the only way to grow and to fend off competitive risks in their increasingly unstable and global marketplaces. It also seems that they aren't pleased by their results so far and remain perplexed about how to foster sustained innovation.

The Boston Consulting Group surveyed 940 executives in 68 countries and concluded that:

> "... successfully managing the innovation process is far from easy—which probably explains one of the most troubling findings from the survey. When executives were asked whether they were satisfied with the financial return on their innovation investments, one out of every two participants worldwide answered no.

> "In the end, it is clear that the biggest challenge in innovation remains **execution**, not invention. Successful innovation is profitable innovation, which depends not just on initial creativity but also on excellent commercialization."

As we have introduced Business Technology Management (BTM) in major corporations and other organizations over the years, we have seen them develop their ability to execute against their strategies and to solve the problems that have plagued them. BTM essentially gets all of a company on the same page, streamlining management processes, generating the information needed to understand what is going on, and replacing previously disjointed efforts with collaboration.

Here is how BTM can enable an organization to be innovative, and to sustain it.

1. The first step in creating an environment of sustained innovation is an assessment of the organization's structure. Reviewing our observations of Xerox/PARC above, an organization aspiring to sustained innovation will need:

- Mechanisms to unite the strategically oriented top of the organization with the tactically oriented bottom

- Mechanisms to foster horizontal collaboration within the organization and across its boundaries with outside partners to identify and assess new opportunities

- Processes that tie business technology investments to business strategy and capture the strategic opportunities created by business technologies

> "You need to establish processes to implement new practices. Coordination is necessary for both invention and implementation, but it happens in different ways. Within a creative work group, coordination emerges naturally. It's implicit in the practice. But implementing creative ideas requires coordinating many different groups. That kind of coordination has to be an explicit process."
>
> —*John Seely Brown*
> *former Chief Scientist, Xerox*

These are natural outcomes of implementing BTM. However, research reveals that fewer than one in five corporations have adopted a business technology governance structure that can deliver these capabilities. Rather, companies have typically focused on governance rights for key business technology decisions. Their attention has been on which of three organization designs would be most appropriate: centralized, decentralized, or federal. In a centralized design, most key business technology decisions are made by the IT function. In a decentralized design, most decisions are made by the business units, with the IT function in an advisory role. The federal design combines elements of both by dispersing authority for specific decisions to the business units and the IT function.

Today we need a better way to manage business technology. Innovation doesn't have to be technical, of course—it could be a new marketing campaign—but increasingly innovation is wrapped up in technology, because the whole organization is wrapped up in technology. Business technology:

- Automates transactions and work processes, generating higher productivity and efficiency. Employees, customers or business partners can access services with speed, convenience, and personalization. Think of customer self-service (self-checkouts at retail stores, Internet check-in for airlines), employee self-service (desktop-based self-procurement, self-management of benefits), and online sales.

- Empowers fast, effective decision-making across the enterprise and its partnership network. Think of decision support tools (for example, data warehousing, data mining, OLAP), intranets for dissemination of best practices, and extranets for rapid sharing of information with business partners. Empowerment enables the goal of being easy to do business with by providing front-end workers with intelligence and decision support in their interactions with customers, business partners, or other external stakeholders. Many of these interactions (for example, in the customer call center) require problem or dispute resolution. Examples of empowerment include decision support scripts for call centers and customer service agents and visibility tools in supply chain and logistics processes.

- Facilitates real-time monitoring of operations and business partners through such practices as daily close, operational alerts, and dashboards with drill-down capabilities. Think of monitoring tools (for example, data warehouses, portals) and enterprise risk-management processes. Business technology enhances transparency of business operations, rapid detection and resolution of management control issues, and accurate reporting of the key metrics of business performance.

Innovation can occur in any of these activities, but on a higher level business technology can enable entirely new business models (for example, direct to the customer, multiple-channel integration, whole of the enterprise or "one face" integration, value net integration), new products and services (for example, digital products and services, digitized customer service through online chats), and new modes of organizing work (for example, globally distributed work practices). The focus here is not so much on specific business technologies as much as on the development of digital options, digitization of products and services, and on experimentation with new business technology-enabled business ideas. Here is the heart of continuous innovation, agility and competitive disruption.

> "I often wonder what new development will come along and totally change the face of our industry. You can be sure it will happen; it's just a question of when and what it is. It can be a new technology, a new operating environment, a new market, or even a new competitor. The most important question at Dell is: Will we be able to identify it? Will we be able to take full advantage of it?"
>
> —Michael Dell
> Chairman, Dell

To realize these benefits of technology, organizations need a more sophisticated organizing logic than they have traditionally employed. The organization's design should encourage business innovation, strategic experiments, and risk-taking with business technology. A *modular* organizing logic provides the structures that can make these things happen. In particular, recalling the importance of collaboration, these structures should nurture three types of networks:

- *Visioning networks* involve senior business and technology executives and the board. They foster collaboration on a strategic vision about the role of business technology. One way to establish a visioning network is to have the CIO as a formal member of the top management team. Other ways include the establishment of a Business Technology Management Council and a Business Technology Investment Board. Boards of directors should also consider establishing their own business technology committees.

- *Innovation networks*, involving business and technology executives, foster collaboration for conceptualizing and implementing business technology applications. These applications are often aimed at enhancing the firm's agility and innovation in customer relationships, manufacturing, product development, supply chain management, or enterprise control and governance systems. One mechanism that promotes innovation networks is corporate and divisional project approval committees. Whereas visioning networks shape overall enterprise perspectives, innovation networks focus on specific innovations and strategic applications.

- *External networks* are relationships with external partners and customers. Their purpose is to foster collaboration between internal and external parties when designing and managing multi-sourcing arrangements, joint ventures, or strategic alliances. Sourcing networks help companies improve their capabilities and business thinking about innovative uses of technology. Attention to sourcing networks must be emphasized in key organizational units that deal with the technical architecture and infrastructure (for example, Office of Architecture and Standards), and the management of technology investments (Enterprise Program Management Office [EPMO]).

Which of these structures to use, who will populate them—and they should include both business and technology executives—and what their specific responsibilities are will vary from firm to firm. They may want to designate individuals or create subcommittees in these groups to focus strictly on innovation. The point is that they are the means through which collaboration becomes systematic. They also become the bodies that collect innovative ideas, evaluate them, and pursue the most promising.

2. With a new organizational design established, the second step is to prepare the people for change. It is not our purpose here to discuss change management in depth, except to say that if the people are not prepared well, success is unlikely. The key components are:

- A comprehensive communications plan to explain the organization's need to be innovative, the role every employee should play and how the new organization will work

- New group and individual goals

- New incentives

Pay attention not just to "the people," but more importantly to the executives in key positions. They have established ways of managing business technology and dealing with the IT function, and these will likely have to change. The executives may well feel threatened and can subtly undermine your best efforts. "Phantom" IT operations are well-known—business technology deployed outside the realm of the IT function by managers unhappy with the service they get.

> "The nub of why alignment is so hard is that, fundamentally, you're talking about cultural change and behavior change in people, and if you have kids and have ever tried to change their behaviors, you can understand how hard that really is at times."
>
> —John Scanlon
> VP, Capital One
> Financial Corporation

3. The new groups next conduct an assessment of the organization's business and technology strategies. First, do they exist in workable detail, beyond broad mission statements? Do they identify the organization's goals, the business capabilities necessary to achieve those goals, and the business technology that will enable those capabilities?

The groups should next conduct a sourcing analysis. What are external partners providing us now? What should we look outside for? Who are the most innovative suppliers of what we need? Cost can be a consideration here, but more important are the top line opportunities to expand into new markets, improve time to market and create a better experience for customers. With these changes, what will the new business model look like? What processes are needed? What will the underlying technology look like?

A customer analysis, likewise, can reveal how the organization is connected to its customers and whether these connections allow the capture of new ideas. What can we learn from our customers, and do we have the technology in place to do so? This can range from website analytics to co-invention with customers. Similarly, is the infrastructure in place to capture ideas from employees? How will that process work? Is technology in place to allow collaboration among far-flung employees in different units and disciplines?

The Business Technology Council and the other new bodies derive the information they need for these analyses from portfolios

"Companies that listen to their customers and respond swiftly with personalized products, solutions or processes can gain an advantage in today's competitive marketplace. However, you can't listen to your customers effectively if your data about them is buried in technology or processes that prevent your employees from having easy and immediate access to that information."

—*Geoff Light*
VP, CRM, UPS

> "We're working extensively on governance process initiatives that allow us to be very easy to do business with from a business partner standpoint. This helps our business partners know how to engage us, so that we have well-honed processes that allow us to be aligned with them. We work hard on initiatives like "Voice of the Customer" to make sure that, with the business, we collect a lot of great requirements from our end customers on what it is that we should build and make sure that we're aligned on, what the priorities are and how we should go about delivering the capabilities that will make FedEx successful."
>
> —*Robert Carter*
> *CIO, FedEx*

that contain all current activity—employees, partners, customers, hard assets such as servers, soft assets such as patents, projects, potential projects and innovative ideas. With these portfolios, the organization can intelligently assess what it would need to pursue a new idea and whether it has the resources on hand, and make such decisions as whether to create a new unit to develop a new idea. Many firms today don't really know what they have. The old story about an employee opening a closet door and discovering a server, and nobody knew what it did, has a good deal of truth in it.

The goal in all of this is to have business and technology decision makers collaborating on ideas flowing continuously from employees, customers and partners. With the big picture in mind, they can evaluate new products and services, new business processes and entirely new business models. There is no guarantee that they will see and act on the next big thing, but creating a process for it makes it much more likely.

Not a copy of its former self

Innovation is alive and well at Xerox today. It invests six percent of revenues in research, development and engineering. In

2005 it brought 49 new products to market. Two-thirds of its equipment sales that year came from products introduced in the past two years.

Two things stand out. One is that Xerox executives and employees spend an enormous amount of time with customers, understanding their needs and providing solutions. The second is that Xerox looks outward, through a panoply of partnerships with corporations, institutes and universities.

And it's a lot less likely that Xerox will experience its PARC fumbles again. Since PARC began to spin off startup companies to take new PARC inventions and run with them, it has started nearly 30 such companies. And Xerox has since spun off PARC itself as a wholly-owned subsidiary. Xerox is a big customer, of course, but PARC scientists now make contributions to non-competing firms.

In other words, for all the product innovation that has gone on there, it might be fair to say that the most valuable innovation at Xerox was the creation of a new business model.

The Nimble Giants

Innovation in big companies. No left turns. Does success breed failure? Organizing for innovation. Managing technology for maximum business effect. It's the customer, stupid. Changing diapers. A new way to build an airliner. Your most important questions.

When a big, brown UPS truck pulls into your driveway, what you see is, well, a big, brown truck. What you don't see is the driver's wireless connection to the global network of one of the world's most innovative companies. It has chosen brown trucks as a symbol, but it has found its competitive edge in business technology.

The destinations of the packages in the truck on your driveway were identified electronically and loaded in the order in which the driver will deliver them. Before that, they were automatically sorted in UPS' mammoth WorldPort air hub in Louisville, Ky. Before that they were launched into the system by senders using UPS' website and its many online tools.

For a little fun, ask the driver how many left turns he made to reach your driveway. UPS has mined its vast store of data to create delivery routes with fewer left-hand turns, which are more time-consuming.

Sustained innovation is in this company's DNA. It shows up in little things, like replacing the cords on hand-held scanners with a wireless connection, because the cords kept breaking. And it shows up in the big things, like transforming UPS from a package delivery company to a global supply chain maestro.

Following the mandate of Founder Jim Casey to be "constructively dissatisfied," UPS has mastered the art of sustained innovation and survived to celebrate its 100th birthday in 2007.

Does success breed failure?

UPS has deftly maneuvered through the innovation paradox: when companies are successful in selling a product or service, they are inclined to dedicate every energy in the organization to maintaining the status quo. The company tinkers with the business, of course, making incremental improvements, but the mindset is to not rock the boat. Why mess with a good thing? The successful company takes in more money and grows larger.

> "Kmart was better than any of us. But it did so well that one of its executives said in the latter part of the '70s that the only way they were vulnerable was if they changed from what they were doing. So they just decreed that no one could change anything. They sat for about five years running stores, but did not change a thing. All of us copied everything they were doing and improved upon it. [Kmart] woke up five years down the road, looked around, and saw there were retailers better than they were. They just never caught up."
>
> —David Glass
> former CEO, Wal-Mart

All is well, right? No.

The drivers of those big brown trucks at UPS will find themselves visiting different companies in the coming years. Analyses of big companies, such as those listed in the Fortune 500, indicate that all is not well. Take the S&P 500. Only 74 of the original 500 companies in 1957 were still on the list 40 years later. That's a mortality rate of more than 10 per year.

QUESTION
Q

How old is your company? How old are your rivals? What is the average life expectancy of a company in your industry?

And the rate is increasing. The average life span of an S&P 500 company has steadily decreased from more than 50 years to fewer than 25 today, according to Langdon Morris, senior practice scholar at the Ackoff Center for the Advancement of Systems Approaches at the University of Pennsylvania. Projecting the pattern forward, he says, it's likely that only about a third of today's major corporations will survive as significant businesses for the next twenty-five years.

Let's make this personal. If you're the CEO of a major company, you might want to keep your resume up to date. CEOs are leaving their jobs at a record rate, and the rate is growing. The consulting firm Booz Allen Hamilton has been tracking the 2,500 largest companies globally for five years. Its latest survey, in 2005, revealed that more than one in seven made a change in leadership, compared with only one in 11 a decade earlier. Four times as many CEOs were forced out in 2005 for under-performance as had been 10 years earlier.

Excuse all the numbers, but they put specificity on the Schumpeterian "creative destruction" all around us. It's real, and it can be measured.

> "The problem that is usually being visualized is how capitalism administers existing structures, whereas the relevant problem is how it creates and destroys them."
>
> —*Joseph Schumpeter*
> *Economist*

And big companies are no more immune than smaller, traditionally high-risk firms. In fact, it is conventional wisdom that small, nimble startups are the fruits of innovation and routinely catch the big guys unaware. The corporate giants, owing to the fact that people are only human, begin focusing on their own navels, develop competencies in internecine warfare, and paralyze themselves with analysis, it being normal human behavior to feather one's nest and resist change.

And so we see big, successful firms get walloped in the marketplace. A college student starts assembling PCs in his dorm room, and eventually his company, Dell, edges IBM out of the business. Not to mention a college dropout named Gates, who out-maneuvers IBM on operating systems. Wal-Mart comes along and venerable Sears Roebuck is wounded, while Kmart bites the dust. Digital photography comes of age, and Kodak's long-term picture loses focus.

On and on we can go with these stories, and you wonder what the people leading these companies were thinking. How could they miss seeing that their world had changed?

On the other hand, such bruises in the marketplace might signal not incompetence but an enthusiasm to be in the fight. IBM, for instance, repeatedly earns more patents than any other company. Its researchers have won five Nobel prizes, six National Medals of Technology and five National Medals of Science. With a hand in just about every area of the digital revolution, IBM is clearly an innovative company. Was it a misstep after all to have abandoned the PC, which had become a commodity? In the title of his book, former Chairman Lou Gerstner asks, "Who Says Elephants Can't Dance?" Indeed, in the frantic speed of today's marketplace, IBM has emerged as the queen of the ball. Don't fixate on individual technologies; keep your eye on your business model.

TASK

Make a list of six ways in which your marketplace has changed in the past two years. What changes are likely in the future?

Big companies have resources the little guys lack. They have established brands, distribution channels and partners. They have groups studying their markets and their strategies, and conducting research on new products. They may have a cash horde to invest in new ideas. They have access to far-flung resources, such as manufacturing and R&D companies in China and India. It is hard to turn a big ship—witness the wrenching transformations at IBM and Kodak—but there is a lot of momentum behind them, even if they are on the wrong course.

Innovative and Big
We can trace several common characteristics of big, innovative firms.

The most important in our view is that they have brought the management of their business and their technology together.

Let's look deeper into UPS as an example. It has been recognized for its innovative thinking, winning such accolades as the "Most Innovative Company" award for the technological advances at its global air hub in Louisville and the "Most IT-enabled Organization of the Year" award.

"For nearly all companies, sustainable growth revolves, in some measure, around determining how technology can be leveraged to enable transformation through innovation."

—David Barnes
CIO, UPS

It's certainly big. It's the world's largest package delivery company. It invests $1 billion a year in technology and owns the world's ninth largest airline. Everyday it moves nearly 15 million packages—or two percent of the world's gross domestic product—through its global network.

The convergence of business and technology at UPS begins with a mindset—it's buried deep in the culture. "IT is an equal player at the strategy table," CIO David Barnes says. "IT and the business are partners in a collaboration-driven strategy."

This convergence takes physical form in the organizational structure. Barnes sits on the Management Committee, the top executive group that oversees operations. He chairs the Program Project Oversight Committee, a cross-functional group through which all projects, technology and otherwise, come for prioritization. And he chairs the IT Governance Committee, which considers all major IT initiatives; it's made up of business and IT people. Presenting to that committee are IT portfolio managers, each of which has a business partner. Other groups study emerging technologies. One is the Information Technology Steering Committee, which looks for innovative uses of new technologies. Only a handful of its 30 members are technologists.

QUESTION
Q

Can your techies talk business? Do your business execs' eyes glaze over when technology comes up?

This cross-function collaboration means that business executives have to become comfortable with evaluating and advocating for technology. And technologists have to learn to talk in business terminology. "Technology ideas can originate from many areas within the company," Barnes says. "It's not territorial. If a marketing person hears something new at a seminar and shares the idea, it's not seen as a challenge but as something we should look at together."

"We need to be focused on where customers are going. We should be playing into major demographic trends and the needs of our customers."

—*Jeffrey Immelt*
Chairman & CEO, GE

Recall the innovation model we outlined in Chapter 3. Corporations will have to define the specific structures they need, their memberships and their roles. There is no one absolute way to do it. The point is that, however they structure it, successful innovators like UPS systematically bring all parts of their organizations together to consider and implement new ideas. Converging the management of business and technology is no guarantee that a company will become innovative. But it is a prerequisite to holistically seeing the inter-related parts of the company and positioning it to seize on opportunities.

Why this is so was revealed in a study of more than 600 mid-sized companies (100 to 500 employees) led by Harvard Business School Professor Marco Iansiti. He and participants from Keystone Strategies and Microsoft chose mid-size companies because their internal workings are easier to analyze. They found that companies that have aligned the design of their business processes and their IT systems can grow revenues and profits faster than other companies:

> "The best firms couple the design of their information technology system with the design of the firm. In each of the case study firms, the design and implementation of critical business processes is tightly integrated with the design and implementation of IT capabilities needed to manage these processes. This integration allows companies to achieve **business processes scalability**. This is a fundamentally different view of scalability than is traditionally used in IT. Classically, IT scalability focuses on things such as the scalability of electronic transactions processing. Here, the corporations focused on using IT to improve the scalability of critical business processes."

In addition to growth in revenues and profits, the researchers found that a well-designed IT infrastructure grants these additional benefits:

- New capabilities and process extensions can be more easily integrated into existing processes.

- Process improvements, through total quality initiatives and employee feedback, are easier to generate, evaluate, and implement.

- Business opportunities can be accessed more quickly and efficiently through the extension of new IT enabled business processes.

- The entire business process portfolio can be more easily monitored and tracked to quickly respond to changes in the business.

With the management of business and technology converged, the organization becomes a seedbed in which new ideas can take root and grow. The organization becomes nimble in exploiting new ideas. Everything can move faster.

Business Model Warfare

Many of the innovations in the overnight delivery business came from UPS rival FedEx, which built the first website on which a transaction could be completed and designed the first package tracking service, among other things. It was FedEx Founder and CEO Frederick Smith who said, back in 1979, "Information about the package will soon be just as important as the delivery of that package." If you're just hauling boxes around in a truck, it's pretty hard to differentiate yourself. And so these companies fight it out on the battlefield of technology innovation.

> "Innovation, which creates sustainable differentiation, is what you want. What most companies do, and why you have the feeling that they're just talking about it, is they innovate but they do not achieve sustainable differentiation. Yes, they're spending a lot on research and development, but at the end of the day, they are not substantially differentiated from their competitors."
>
> —Geoffrey Moore
> Author

No less than UPS, FedEx manages its technology for maximum business effect. Recognizing the strategic nature of business technology, the FedEx board of directors has created a committee devoted to it. CIO Robert Carter sits on the Executive Committee and Strategic Management Committee. A key part of his role is working with his business colleagues to understand the needs of their customers.

If you focus on the whizbang technology in these companies, you will miss the more important message—that they use technology not just to speed up processes but also to create competitive advantage in new business models. UPS is now using its technology and the information it generates to become a supply chain manager for other companies. New business models are where the action is, because that's where the value is. And that's what makes converging the management of business and the management of technology so critical. A company can't successfully change one without changing the other.

How Companies Learn
Innovative companies connect their employees, customers and partners so as to learn from them and capture new ideas. They do this by creating the visioning, innovation and outside networks discussed in Chapter 3. These firms establish flows of information to and from these groups and have in place processes to discover and deploy the ideas floating along in those flows.

"A majority of executives believe that high-quality relationships with outside parties will become more important as a source of competitive advantage between now and 2020. Collaborative problem-solving is expected to increase in volume inside and outside the organization, as customers and suppliers become more involved in product development, as cross-functional and cross-border teams work together more frequently and as partnerships with other organizations proliferate."

—Foresight 2020 Survey
Economist
Intelligence Unit

Employees—At first glance it would appear that the strategy at many companies renowned for their innovation is to just let a thousand flowers bloom. Take W.L. Gore & Associates, best known for its waterproof and windproof fabrics. A few years ago *Fast Company* magazine pronounced W.L. Gore "pound for pound, the most innovative company in America."

> "It's extremely important to have systems and processes because there are two levels at which innovation takes place. First, there is the freewheeling environment, the open environment, with discussions, debates, etc. But second, in order to make sure that those ideas are actually market worthy and that the corporation is in a position to leverage those ideas, you need systems and processes. They compress the cycle time and maximize the returns on those ideas."
>
> —*N.R. Narayana Murthy*
> *Co-Founder, Infosys*

To understand why, *Fast Company* explored the company in-depth. Gore actually has more than a 1,000 products, ranging from artificial blood vessels to guitar strings, created by its employees, who are encouraged to spend 10 percent of their time on purely speculative ideas. Consider the origins of Elixir, Gore's guitar string, which is the top-selling acoustic string. Dave Myers, an engineer in the medical products division, who had created various plastic heart implants, was trying to improve the gear cables on his mountain bike. He coated them with a thin layer of plastic, which worked, leading to a new Gore product. Next he decided to improve the cables used in amusement parks to drive big animated puppets. To experiment, he played around with guitar strings, and then it dawned on him: why wouldn't this be good for the guitar strings themselves?

He was joined by another colleague, a guitarist, and they worked for several years with no success. Then they were joined by yet another engineer, who had worked on the successful launch of a new dental floss. He began work on the guitar strings in his spare time; his day job was creating a new inventory management system for doctors and hospitals.

This ultimately successful collaboration was loose and spontaneous but not random. Gore has created an environment in which creative people work in small, multi-disciplinary teams with a minimum of command and control hierarchy. Yet it turns their ideas into profitable products. Gore may provide a fertile field where a thousand flowers can bloom, but it knows how to pick only the best. For one thing, employees must enlist the support of others, and truly cock-eyed ideas are not going to get support. Two, everyone is evaluated on the basis of past performance and future promise, so employees' use of free time to speculate is reviewed regularly. Finally, of course, promising ideas must be presented to and approved by management.

One of the most interesting things about Gore is that it is as innovative in its business models as in its products. When retailers refused to carry the guitar strings because they were three times the price of regular strings, Gore gave away 20,000 samples in one year to subscribers of guitar magazines. The strings now have a 35 percent share of the market. Gore did the same thing with its Glide dental floss, giving it away to dentists. And the fact that you even know about Gore is the result of its innovative marketing idea—to put a Gore-Tex tag on garments made of its fabric. This is reminiscent of Intel's "Intel Inside" sticker on PCs.

Google looks a lot like Gore. It's a flat organization, employees can spend 20 percent of their time pursuing their instincts, teams are small, there is no micromanagement. It throws off a seemingly endless array of dazzling products. More interesting, however, is how Google's business model has evolved, from simple search engine to advertising powerhouse, all the while expanding its offerings and assuming a larger role in the daily lives of its users.

Customers—We can see in UPS several other characteristics of innovative companies. One is that innovation is driven by their customers. UPS is literally in the face of its customers—accessible via the Web on anyone's computer. The company studies the millions of visits to UPS.com each day to identify new products and services to offer. Dell does the same thing with its corporate customers, creating customized websites that allow individuals to make purchases based on their company's specifications. Yahoo is hiring economists to mine data on the activities of its 500 million Web visitors each month.

It is interesting to note how these companies use technology to keep themselves in front of more and more customers. UPS extends itself, for example, through Amazon's website to allow Amazon's customers to track the delivery of their purchases. Amazon extends itself through numerous websites to allow visitors to make purchases. Google inserts itself into websites to provide site-specific and general Web searches. All are staying in front of the final customer with a branded presence that works to the benefit of everyone.

As everyone accumulates the same technology to automate internal processes and squeeze out inefficiencies, and as commoditization spreads its destruction, it will become increasingly important to learn from customers. This will become one of the last remaining opportunities for finding a competitive edge. Companies will have to be innovative in how they observe and listen to their customers and how they serve them.

At P&G, CEO A.G. Lafley has been known to visit customers in their homes, in the guise of a market researcher, to observe how P&G's products are used. Other P&G execs do the same— watching people clean floors, wash clothes and diaper babies. The head of the baby care division even opened a diaper testing center just down from her office; there P&G technicians diaper customers' babies and learn.

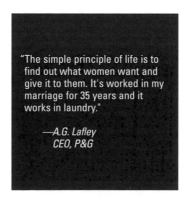

"The simple principle of life is to find out what women want and give it to them. It's worked in my marriage for 35 years and it works in laundry."

—*A.G. Lafley*
CEO, P&G

What does your organization do to understand its customers?

Let's establish a rule: if you want to sell diapers you'd better get out there and change some yourself. (Whoever said business was easy?) On the other hand, you may want to join Design Continuum Inc. A few years ago this West Newton, Mass., design firm videotaped people taking showers (in swim suits) to help Moen Inc. develop a new showerhead.

Research has established that in many fields, much innovation is the handiwork of the end user of a product. As an example, Eric von Hippel, Professor and Head of the Innovation and Entrepreneurship Group at the MIT Sloan School of Management, studied the development of four scientific instruments. End users were the developers of fully 77 percent of the innovations in these instruments.

Von Hippel has developed the concept of the "lead user." Lead users face needs today that will be widespread in the marketplace months or years down the road. They are also positioned to benefit significantly by finding solutions to their problems. And so they tinker with a product to improve it. If the manufacturer can connect with these lead users, and there are ways to do that, the manufacturer can often incorporate these innovations in future versions of the product. Surprisingly, the user-innovator is often willing to give up the idea, because he or she has no financial interest in developing it. Many would be glad to have the manufacturer develop their ideas.

A few years ago Von Hippel worked with 3M to introduce the lead user concept into the company. 3M's $100 million surgical drapes business was stagnating; one reason was that medical insurance wouldn't cover 3M's technically sophisticated but expensive drapes. The unit had not had a breakthrough product in a decade. The company recognized that incremental improvements in existing products wouldn't be enough—3M need something entirely new.

A team was formed, and it set about visiting operating rooms in developing nations. Team members learned that in many places doctors couldn't afford surgical drapes and used antibiotics instead —a long-term problem as microbes become drug-resistant. Working with the surgeons, the team came up with several new ideas, some of which had nothing to do with surgical drapes, such as an antimicrobial coating for tubes and catheters. 3M had previously only dealt with surface infections; this idea would move the company into urinary tract and other internal infections. The team also discovered that what doctors wanted was different types of anti-infection treatment for different types of patients, something 3M's one-size-fits-all drapes didn't offer.

The team realized that it had not only come up with breakthrough products; it had also uncovered a new business model, which the company agreed to adopt. This is an excellent illustration of the fact that that the real action today is in new business models.

The lead user concept spread to other divisions of 3M, and a group of academics from several universities analyzed the results, comparing products resulting from the lead user approach to those developed under traditional market research approaches. Here's what the assessors found:

> *"Annual sales of lead user product ideas generated for the average lead user project at 3M are conservatively projected to be $146 million after 5 years— more than eight times higher than sales for the average contemporaneously-conducted "traditional" project. Each funded lead user project created a new major product line for a 3M division. As a direct result, divisions funding lead user project ideas experienced their highest rate of major product line generation in the past 50 years."*

Staples has gone down another path. It lets customers submit new product ideas, which Staples then develops and sells in its stores. Or consider Netflix. Looking for improvements in its collaborative filtering software that recommends movies to its customers, it is offering a $1 million prize to anyone who improves the current system by 10 percent. "You can be a mathematician in

Romania or a statistician in Taiwan, and you could be the winner," Netflix CEO Reed Hastings said.

Partners—You can do the math—there are far more smart and creative people outside of your company than inside. Successful companies today are looking for innovation beyond their walls. Spending on internal R&D departments is shrinking. At IBM, its famed researchers are now meeting and working directly with customers on innovative solutions to real world problems. At P&G, a new division of employees who once worked on the inside are now sent out to find and partner with innovative companies on new products and technologies. Big companies are setting up R&D centers in China, India and elsewhere at an astonishing rate. This is not your father's outsourcing. This is finding, not the cheapest, but the smartest firms to join your value chain. And it takes many different forms.

TASK

List the companies in your industry that have created significant partner networks. What advantage do they derive from this?

Boeing, for example, has partnered with firms all over the world to not only build but also design the parts of its new 787 "Dreamliner," a 250-seat airplane. Altogether some 135 partner sites in two dozen countries are involved. Fuji Heavy Industries in Japan, for instance, is designing and building the center wing box; Kawasaki is building the main landing gear wheel well. Their work is brought together, not in wooden mockups in Seattle, but virtually in software from Dassault Systems in France. This design system will show whether the pieces work together. Other collaborative technologies are used to track the work and allow the designers to communicate with each other 24/7.

One partner is Vought Aircraft Industries Inc., of Dallas, Texas, which is building two sections of the 787 fuselage. It is working with another firm, Alenia Aeronautica S.p.A., in Italy to integrate pieces of the fuselage. Vought says that this collaborative way of working has taken one-third to one-half out of the time previously required to do such work and has saved probably 50 percent in development costs. Boeing will haul the finished pieces from these widely distributed builders to central assembly plants using specially outfitted 747s. Boeing estimates that final assembly will take only three days, compared to the traditional three weeks.

> "We want to use the best and brightest anywhere in the world, and part of our role at Boeing Technology is finding them. We're seeking Indian ingenuity, or Japanese or British or Italian ingenuity. The mathematicians in Russia are fascinating to talk to, they're trained differently, they think about models and use wind tunnels differently. A big problem, where there is not a lot of structure, we tend to give to the Russians. A big problem with lots of structure, and a chance for continuous improvement, we tend to give to India."
>
> —*Scott Griffin*
> *CIO, Boeing*

Boeing draws on its own internal teams of engineers, of course. It also draws on hundreds of Russian scientists in its engineering design and technical research centers in Moscow. It sought further design input from the financial community: what design features would give the 787 a better resale value? Finally, it opened itself up to the public, creating a World Design Team, in which 120,000 aviators and aviation enthusiasts could contribute their ideas. The name Dreamliner, in fact, was voted on by nearly half a million people around the world. Randy Baseler, vice president of marketing for Boeing Commercial Airplanes, even runs a blog on which he answers queries from ordinary flyers about such design features as electronic window shades.

This is a new, technology-enabled business model. The central organization has created networks that bring its suppliers, knowledge centers and customers into collaboration. Each brings new

> "Customers used to participate in
> design two or three years back.
> But starting last year, many just
> take our product. Because of
> price competition, they have to."
>
> —Jack Hsieh
> *VP, Premiere Imaging*
> *Technology Corp.,*
> *speaking on digital cameras*
> *sold to major companies*

ideas about the 787. Boeing has moved away from top down command and control—you will build a wing precisely this way—to decentralized decision-making—here's the kind of wing we need, you figure it out.

Other companies have adopted variations on this approach. Chances are good, for example, that your PDA, cell phone or laptop was not only manufactured in Asia, but also designed there. Asian companies such as Quanta Computer, Flextronics and Cellon are moving into the design of products, offering such big names as Dell and Motorola a complete soup to nuts product. It's not hard to understand. Why should two competing phone companies each spend $30 million to develop a new phone, given that the innards will basically be the same? Moreover, the Asian supplier can customize the plastic shell and handle other bothersome tasks. For other than high-end, leading-edge differentiating products it just makes sense.

Other companies are following a tack somewhat similar to Boeing by turning to innovation networks. Li & Fung is a Hong Kong company with a network of 7,500 suppliers in 40 countries. These suppliers specialize in garments and other products. Need a line of shirts? Li & Fung will find the right group of companies to design, develop, manufacture and deliver. Since it has no production facilities of its own, the company can constantly employ firms on the basis of the quality, cost and speed.

This is the look of partnerships in the 21st Century. Companies are no longer seeing business technology as a means to reduce bottom line costs. They see it as the source of top line growth. In the same way, outsourcing no longer means throwing off routine tasks on a cheap provider. It is, instead, a knitting together of the best and the brightest, wherever they are, in a network to create value.

Is this for you? It's a strategic question. Where do you need to be innovative? If you are Dell, your innovation is in your supply and delivery processes, so you have more freedom to enlist others to help in product design and development. If you are Motorola, you might let others design your lower-end products, but keep the design of your high-end phone in house. The more commodity-like your product, the less you risk in sending it out. With a competitive differentiator, however, you have more need to retain control.

Do you aim to penetrate an overseas market? Then design and development firms in the countries you are targeting may be a good bet. They can probably help you create products that are appropriately priced for those markets. Beware that the business models these companies put together to reach developing markets are likely to affect the developed world as well; a more efficient and lower cost model will ultimately challenge less efficient and higher cost models in the developed world. And then there's this: what if the company doing your design and manufacturing decides to put its own brand on its work? Will it now become a competitor? Finally, what must be done to prepare your people, organization, processes and technology infrastructure for a networked approach?

The Risk of Innovation

Apple is universally cited as an innovative company, lately on the basis of its iPod. But does anyone remember the Newton, Apple's failed personal digital assistant? Or does anyone recall that Apple co-founder Steve Wozniak, who created the Apple I and Apple II computers, then left Apple to form his own company to make the first universal remote control—which flopped?

There are no guarantees in innovation. Most outsourcing deals fail eventually, most IT projects fail, most startup companies fail and most new products fail. It is not surprising that the list of companies failing with innovative, technology-enabled business models seems almost limitless:

Iridium — the satellite telephone company that entered bankruptcy in 1999, citing a failure to attract subscribers and competition from much improved cell phone service.

Long-Term Capital Management — a hedge fund, whose electronic black box couldn't keep up with rapid changes in the real world's financial markets.

Enron — the trading company whose new business models and high technology created more smoke than profits.

Webvan — the grocery delivery company, whose spending on high-tech gear seemed to exceed its customers spending on groceries.

Now those were smart people, some of the best and brightest in industry. How do we avoid their fate? Perhaps in answer to this unanswerable question we can pose other questions. The management guru Peter Drucker was famed for asking very simple questions when he went into an organization, such as, "Why are we here?" and "What needs to be done?"

His five most important questions, according to one observer, were:

1. *What is the mission?*
2. *Who is the customer?*
3. *What does the customer value?*
4. *What are our results?*
5. *What is our plan?*

"You will see some failures. As we take more risks, this is something we must accept as part of the regeneration process."

—*E. Neville Isdell*
Chairman and CEO
The Coca-Cola Company

"A lot of bad leadership comes from an inability or unwillingness to ask questions. I have watched talented people—people with much higher IQs than mine—who have failed as leaders. They can talk brilliantly, with a great breadth of knowledge, but they're not very good at asking questions. So while they know a lot at a high level, they don't know what's going on way down in the system. Sometimes they are afraid of asking dumb questions, but what they don't realize is that the dumbest questions can be very powerful."

—Mike Parker
President and CEO
Dow Chemical

Not bad. But let's adapt them for our purposes and try to keep them just as simple:

1. *Does the customer really need what you're offering? How do you know?*

2. *Can your partners supply what you need in a cost-effective way?*

3. *Is your organization prepared to make the offering? Are your technology and business people working together on the plan?*

4. *Can competitors meet the customer's need in a simpler, cheaper way? Are you tracking them?*

5. *What can go wrong? Is every voice in your organization being heard, including those you don't want to hear?*

In his book, *Innovation and Entrepreneurship*, Peter Drucker describes Ford Motor Company's failed Edsel as one of the best planned and researched vehicles ever. And yet it flopped almost immediately. Ford's reaction, Drucker writes, was not to find someone else to blame but rather to go out into the marketplace and discover what went wrong. What had happened was a very real but hidden shift in self-perception by automobile buyers, from being in an income segment—a market rationale used by the industry for years—to being in a "lifestyle" segment. Ford responded with the amazingly popular Thunderbird.

As a writer for The Associated Press, one of the hardest things I [Terry Kirkpatrick] had to learn was to ask dumb questions. Nobody wants to appear ignorant, but every new assignment thrust me into an environment I knew little about. Whether it was the bond market or nuclear power, I had to be able to admit that I didn't understand even the basics. I once interviewed the economist Lester Thurow. Beforehand I read everything he had written. I showed up at his office at MIT, and we had a pleasant conversation. When I returned to my office, however, I had nothing to write, because I hadn't asked the personal, penetrating questions that would have enlightened and brought a fresh perspective on his work.

Drucker describes innovation as a delicate dance between perception and analysis. Analysis, with all its discipline, must be based on a perception of change, he writes: "This requires a willingness to say, "I don't actually know enough to analyze, but I shall find out. I'll go out, look around, ask questions, and *listen.*'"

In an age of unanswerable questions, asking the right question might just be the answer.

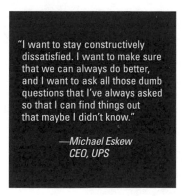

"I want to stay constructively dissatisfied. I want to make sure that we can always do better, and I want to ask all those dumb questions that I've always asked so that I can find things out that maybe I didn't know."

—*Michael Eskew*
CEO, UPS

Social Enterprises Lead the Way

Doing well by doing good. How do you afford a water buffalo? Buddy, can you spare $94? Here comes the motoman. No phones, but "we've got mail!" Saving the okra crop.

In the summer of 2006 I [Faisal Hoque] returned to my native Bangladesh for the first time in 15 years. Nearly half of the country's population of 135 million still lives below the poverty line, but I could also see signs of progress, particularly in the innovative work of Professor Mohammad Yunus.

I knew Professor Yunus from the BTM Institute, an organization that promotes the convergence of business and technology, and we spent an afternoon in Dhaka at his offices. We discussed the critical role of technology in organizations today, and in particular how Professor Yunus has used technology to create new organizational models that help to alleviate the plight of the poor. He pioneered the concept of "microcredit," in which very small loans are made to the poor to help them start or develop a simple business. My visit came just a few months before he was awarded the Nobel Peace Prize for his microcredit innovations.

Estimates are that villagers who have taken advantage of Professor Yunus' microcredit initiative have a household income that is 50 percent higher than non-participants, he told me that afternoon. Only 20 percent of participants are still below the poverty line, compared to 56 percent of non-participants. Clearly this is working as a social initiative, but the amazing thing is that these micro loans are profitable for the bank he launched to manage them. His is a "social enterprise"—a hybrid organization that does well by doing good. Social enterprises earn profits from what was previously considered non-profit activity.

They are worth a deeper look because they have to be innovative to solve the problems they care about. The existing business model in banking, for instance, just could not do what Professor Yunus wanted to do. Old business models in other industries like telecommunications just couldn't relate to people earning less than a dollar a day, and yet there they are, billions of them, the largest untapped market on the globe. How can they be served?

QUESTION

What market do you assume to be impenetrable? Why?

Let's follow the story of Professor Yunus to better understand what's going on here.

Deeply troubled by the thousands of deaths in Bangladesh during a famine in 1974, Yunus, an economics professor at Chittagong University, walked off campus one day and into the neighboring village of Jobra. His purpose was to learn "poor people's economics."

He soon came upon Sufiya Begum, a widow with three children, a landless peasant, one of 55 million in Bangladesh. She made bamboo stools and sold them, for a profit of just two cents a day. She was under the control of a trader, who supplied her with bamboo, but who also required her to sell her output back to him for the miniscule profit.

As Yunus questioned her, he realized that with the equivalent of just 22 cents a day, she could break the hold of the trader, buy the bamboo she needed, and sell her stools for much more than a daily profit of two cents.

TASK

Assume that you had to market your product or service in a developing country, where incomes are very low. How would you do it?

Yunus approached a local banker and asked him to lend her money, but the banker just laughed in his face. The idea of lending such small amounts to a poor woman with no collateral was preposterous. The cost of the paperwork alone would be more than any profit the bank could make.

So Yunus decided to turn the economics of banking on its head. He started his own bank to make tiny loans to poor people. The concept caught fire, and today thousands of "microfinance" organizations are lending billions of dollars to millions of the downtrodden around the world. And many of these organizations are making a profit doing it. Big global financial institutions like Citigroup and ABN Amro Holding have invested millions through these microfinance organizations.

And Yunus' Grameen (the Bengali word for "village") Bank now operates 2,185 branches in 69,140 rural villages, providing credit to 6.4 million of Bangladesh's poorest people. This allows them to make money by husking rice, repairing machines, purchasing rickshaws, and buying milk cows, goats, cloth, and pottery for their simple businesses. Over the years Grameen has lent more than US $5.5 billion—and it has an astounding repayment rate of 98.49 percent.

What does all this mean for us?

The first takeaway is that Grameen Bank was an innovative business model created in response to a genuine human need. As we explored in Chapter 4, businesses are increasingly studying their customers to understand their real needs and then creating models that will meet those needs. The Grameen Bank's first principle is, "Start with the problem rather than the solution: a credit system must be based on a survey of the social background rather than on a pre-established banking technique." Professor Yunus' stroll through a village to learn how people live is in some ways reminiscent of P&G CEO Lafley visiting a customer's home and looking around in the bathroom to see how his products are used. I [Faisal Hoque] am reminded as well of our work at GE, which created an innovative business model and innovative technology, but which offered something out customers didn't want.

A second key insight is that the work of Grameen and other such organizations is made feasible by business technology— 1,756 of Grameen's branches have computerized accounting and management information systems. Only with such automation can these organizations manage the hundreds of thousands of micro-transactions conducted in person by bank representatives with remote villagers. The technology enables the business model.

Innovative uses of technology can be found at SKS Microfinance, a firm started by Vikram Akula, who did graduate work at Yale University and began working with several microfinance organizations in India in 1995. His firm developed soft-

> "In three major areas information and communications technology (ICT) can play an immediate role helping the poor:
>
> 1) integrating the poor into the mainstream economy by expanding their market, eliminating the middlemen in their business, and creating international job opportunities through service outsourcing;
>
> 2) bringing information, educational programmes, skills training, and healthcare services, etc., all in a very user friendly way, even to the most remote villages;
>
> 3) empowering the poor, particularly poor women, with a stronger voice that can be heard behind the borders of their village, better access to information, and improvement in the democratic process."
>
> —*Professor Muhammad Yunus*

"I think software executives should realize the strong role IT plays in the development sector, especially microfinance. The importance of IT in microfinance cannot be understated. For example, the development of an MIS system and various software modules have allowed and will allow us to drastically reduce the cost of our operations. Microfinance, as an industry, is looking at ways to increase the scalability and efficiency of microfinance institutions through the use of biometrics, smart card PDAs, POS devices, and integrated software technologies—all which will help us better deliver financial services to our clientele."

—*Vikram Akula*
CEO and Founder
SKS Microfinance

ware with a number of features, one of the more important being a graphical user interface that anyone can learn quickly — most of the company's field staff have a limited education and little or no computer experience. The system tracks each transaction so that corporate staffers can quickly spot problems in the field. And it has an online data transfer capability that allows it to send transaction information back to the head office daily. All branch level transactions are consolidated and compressed so that they can be sent over a dial-up connection in less than 2 minutes.

Akula has been innovative, as well, with his business processes. When a field staffer visits a village to collect payments, all loan recipients are expected to be in one place at the same time, to save the staffer from having to track them down. They repay the same amount each time in multiples of five rupees to avoid having to make change. With these efficiencies and the technology, SKS is able to pay the staff and eke out a 1-2 percent profit, which it plows back into the business. The company says that 63 of the world's top microfinance institutions have an average rate of return of about 2.5% of total assets.

S.K. Pahima is one of SKS' success stories. Divorced at 21, with two small children and living with her father, she received a loan of $175, with which she purchased five bicycles. She rented them out for seven cents an hour. Another loan, for $44, allowed her to purchase three more bikes. Soon she was making $131 a month and repaying her loans. When an SKS branch opened up in her village, she applied for a job as loan officer and was hired. She now manages 20 loan groups, which have 605 clients and $64,200 in loans outstanding.

For its part, Grameen Bank made a profit of $15.21 million in 2005. All of it was transferred to a Rehabilitation Fund created to cope with disaster situations; this fulfilled a condition imposed by the government for exempting Grameen Bank from paying corporate income tax.

In addition to their business model and business process innovations, these firms are innovative in products. Grameen, for example, has made 635,900 housing loans averaging $190. It grants scholarships and provides education loans. Borrowers get free life insurance. It has created a pension fund for its borrowers. The bank has a special program for beggars, with very liberal loan provisions to help them move from begging to selling consumer products; they even get free life insurance.

Over the years Professor Yunus has created a number of for-profit and not-for-profit companies, most of them focused on using technology for the greater good of the poor in Bangladesh. There's a software company, an Internet services provider, a fund to finance risky, technology-oriented ventures, and two telephone companies.

> "I'm deeply convinced that our future relies on our ability to explore and invent new business models and new types of business corporations."
>
> —Franck Riboud
> Chairman and CEO
> Groupe Danone, which has partnered with Grameen to provide nutritious, low-cost foods in Bangladesh

The Facts of Poverty

- **1.2 billion** people worldwide live on less than one dollar/day adjusted to purchasing power parity (PPP)
- **1 billion** other people live below the poverty line of 2 dollars
- **80% of the world's population** does not have access to credit; 500-600 million of these people would be eligible for microcredit.
- **Over 80 million** people are now assisted by over 10,000 micro-finance institutions.
- **54.8 million** of these people are among the poorest popula-tions. These 54.8 million people and their 274 million family members is equal to the populations of Great Britain, France, Germany, Italy, Ireland and Sweden.

—PlaNet Finance
an NGO dedicated to using microfinance
to assist the poor

One of these phone companies is the non-profit Grameen Telecom. It buys mobile phone airtime from Grameen Phone, whose majority owner is Norway's Telenor. The non-profit firm goes into a village and selects from among Grameen Bank's cus-tomers a woman to manage the "village phone." She sets up an office or kiosk, sells call time to villagers, retains some of the rev-enue as her profit, and returns the rest to the company. It's a good deal for the villagers, the "telephone ladies," as Professor Yunus refers to them, and for the companies. Although the program is altruistic in mission, Jon Fredrik Baksaas, CEO and President of Telenor, has told us that this is one of his company's fastest grow-ing markets and has one of the company's highest gross profit margins. Today 200,000 telephone ladies are earning good incomes for their families and contributing $11 million a month in revenue to Grameen Phone.

In 2006 Professor Yunus was awarded the "ITU World Information Society Award" by the International Telecommunication Union. "I do not come from a technology background," he said in

Do you listen to your younger, more idealistic employees about their passions?

his acceptance speech. "I got interested in information and communication technology because I saw this as a powerful new technology which can help the poor people, particularly poor women, out of poverty very fast. All you need to do is to find a business model where ICT can become an income-generating opportunity to the poor."

But something more is going on here than just raising the daily income of poor people. These isolated villagers, using village phones to learn about market conditions or get information from the government, are being connected to the global knowledge economy. As they use such information as market prices for their produce to better their lot, they are also becoming a more attractive market.

Many other organizations are using technology innovatively to help make those connections. An Indian company called n-Logue, for instance, has created a business model somewhat similar to Grameen's to bring wireless voice and Internet connections to remote villages. At the top is n-Logue, which handles regulatory and connectivity issues. In the middle are Local Service Providers, which find subscribers and collect payments. At the bottom are the village kiosks.

These kiosks have been used for a variety of purposes—"town hall" type meetings with government officials, to get medical care needed by villagers and to get advice on crop disease from an agricultural college. In the last case, a village's entire okra crop was threatened. Using a photo from the kiosks web cam, the college diagnosed the disease and suggested a treatment, saving the $3,300 crop.

The rugged PC

One interesting strategy for connecting isolated villages involves innovative uses of PCs, satellite Internet connections and wireless technology. In Cambodia, for instance, motorcycle riders make the rounds in isolated villages that have no electrical or telephone connections to the outside world. On the back of the cycles is a wireless-enabled computer. As the driver, called a "motoman," approaches a school, he slows down, and the wireless device communicates with a solar-powered PC in the school. Email and Web browsing requests from villagers are collected by the motorcycle computer, which then transmits email and Web sites to the school's computer.

> "In 1999, my wife and I built two (of what have since become five) schools in Cambodia and brought broadband Internet into villages that had no electricity, no telephone, no television, no running water and (in the case of one village) no road. Our son installed WiFi and brought laptops that the kids took home at night. Parents loved this because the laptops were the brightest light source in the house and the portability was obviously very compelling as well. It's also interesting to note that the first English word each child learned was Google."
>
> —*Nicholas Negroponte*
> *Chairman, MIT Media Lab*

Off the motorcycle goes to the next village, and eventually it reaches a satellite uplink, where it passes on the villagers' newest emails. It's asynchronous and once a day, but it works. This system is the handiwork of Bernard Krisher, a retired journalist who created American Assistance for Cambodia, an NGO that has raised money to build schools in the country.

Robib, Cambodia, is a collection of six tiny, nearly inaccessible villages with no plumbing, electricity or telephones. The average annual income here is just $40 a year. But Robib has a donated PC powered by solar panels. A corporation has lent the village a satellite dish to connect to the Internet, and the villagers have made the most of it. They have created a Web site (www.villageleap.com), where they sell silk scarves and neckties woven by villagers, who

"First and foremost is AMD's 50x15 vision of providing 50 percent of the world's population with Internet access by 2015. Such a level of technology penetration would serve to help educate children worldwide. Subsequent benefits to AMD might include a new high volume channel for low-power processor solutions, software maturation and development, and new innovations that arise during the development of the product. This approach is built upon incentives and strategies that are not just about goodwill but also about good business."

—*Hector Ruiz*
Chairman and CEO, AMD

have resurrected the land's ancient skill in silk weaving, lost under the Khmer Rouge regime.

Big companies are looking for ways to enter these developing markets. They are seeking "strategies that are not just about goodwill but also about good business," AMD Chairman and CEO Hector Ruiz says. AMD's "50x15" program has the ambitious goal of connecting 50 percent of the world population by the year 2015. One of its many contributions to this is the Personal Internet Communicator (PIC), an inexpensive, rugged, simplified PC-like device that can connect to the Internet for email and Web browsing.

AMD has partnered with Cable & Wireless, an international provider of IP, voice and data services, to make the PIC available in the Caribbean. C&W bundles the PIC with high-speed Internet service. It realized that its customers were buying high-end cell phones and that if it could provide a PC at the same price as a phone, people might buy it. C&W also realized that for many people, individual ownership of the device wasn't possible or necessary. And so its business model is based not on ownership but on public access — in Internet cafes, schools, hospitals and other public places. "Broadband is changing business models for ISPs," says Enrique Camacho, Sr. Vice President of Internet and Data,

Caribbean, Cable & Wireless. "Ten years ago, broadband was not available, but it is now. And AMD is working with us to pioneer this new broadband model in the Caribbean."

AMD's archrival, Intel, also has big plans for the developing world. It will spend $5 billion on several initiatives, including a low-price PC that is resistant to dust and heat and can run off a car battery. "This clearly is viewed by us as being good for the world and good for Intel," CEO Paul Otellini has said. "There is a solid commercial payoff for it."

One of the leading voices encouraging companies to invest in developing countries is C.K. Prahalad, the Paul and Ruth McCracken Distinguished University Professor of Corporate Strategy at the University of Michigan's Roth School of Business. He is an acclaimed consultant to major corporations on strategy and is considered one of the top business thinkers in the world. In his book, *The Fortune at the Bottom of the Pyramid: Eradicating Poverty through Profits*, he argues that,

> *"What is needed is a better approach to help the poor, an approach that involves partnering with them to innovate and achieve sustainable win-win scenarios where the poor are actively engaged and, at the same time, the companies providing products and services to them are profitable. If large firms approach this market with bottom of the pyramid consumers' interests at heart, it can also lead to significant growth and profits for them."*

Grameen's "do well by doing good" model has spawned other business innovations, such as intermediary firms that connect the world's capital markets to microfinance organizations. Alexandre de Lesseps runs investment firms that do this. "You're not going to get rich investing in microfinance," he says. "But at the same time, it's safer than the stock market and offers a much better return than a typical money market account. If you're a blue-chip investor sitting on a lot of cash, it makes sense to put up to 4 percent of your net worth into this type of fund. You also get the satisfaction of knowing that your money is doing good for the poor people of the world."

Spawning innovations

Yet another innovative finance idea was the brainstorm of Matthew and Jessica Flannery, she a staffer with the Village Enterprise Fund, he a filmmaker. Working together in Kenya, Tanzania and Uganda, and observing small entrepreneurs, they came up with the idea for Kiva, a company that allows individuals in the developed world to loan money to entrepreneurs in the developing world. Those seeking funding make their pitch on Kiva's website (www.kiva.org), where potential lenders, sitting at home in the United States in front of a PC, can lend as little at $25 using PayPal. These aren't gifts; they are loans to be repaid, although they are repaid without interest.

One beneficiary is Michael Ewalu, a dairy farmer in Soroti, Uganda, and the father of four. Ewalu borrowed $2,000 through Kiva in 2005 to purchase two cows and a bull of a better breed than what he owned. The new cows give more milk, and with the profits Ewalu has repaid $530 of his loan.

You can be sitting in your family room in, say, Ohio, your laptop wirelessly connected to the Internet, and for as little as $25 you can invest in a dairy farm in Uganda. Or, for just $15, buy a hand woven necktie, or for $22 a hand woven scarf, from a villager in Robib, Cambodia. (They also sell coffee, cotton bags and paper products.) Hey, delight your spouse this Christmas! From the comfort of your easy chair!

"One common view of business makes a sharp distinction between making money and doing good in society. This is a limited and distorted perspective. Business that focuses just on money doesn't invest in the future—in its employees, new ideas, markets or products—and won't be around for long. Any successful business is part of society and exists to meet society's needs."

—Lord John Browne
Group Chief Executive
British Petroleum

"Innovation always leads
you down paths people think
are weird."

—*Jeff Bezos*
CEO, Amazon

These things don't surprise us anymore, because we are accustomed to discovering nearly everyday some new clever thing we can do with technology.

And yet something profound is going on here. To understand it, should we resort to buzzwords, and say that we are all now nodes on the edge of a global network? That technology has eliminated distance, not just between here and Cambodia, but also the nine and a half hours it takes to drive from Robib to Phnom Penh? That big things happen today through a blend of non-profit, for-profit and government organizations? That the economics we took for granted has been turned on its head?

Should we just call on the term we've repeatedly used in this book: new, technology-enabled business models?

The takeaway for anyone in a for-profit, non-profit, or government organization is that if you can identify a genuine need, you have at your disposal today the technology to meet it. The heavy

"We need people who can combine passion with process. Schools like Cornell and places like GE are excellent at teaching process. But we both need to do more to give people a sense of how it feels to win and lose—and to have the passion that makes them want to see their visions become reality more than anybody else.

—*Jeffrey Immelt*
Chairman & CEO, GE

lifting comes in a creating an appropriate business model. To do that you have to see things differently.

For those in a corporate, for-profit organization, we think two concepts can be drawn from the stories in this chapter.

Who needs what?

The first is a rethinking of the meaning of "need." Abraham Maslow, the psychologist, is famed for his "hierarchy of needs," a framework expressing the idea that human beings have a set order of needs: water and food come first, then security, and ultimately "self-actualization." People who are hungry are not too worried about self-actualization. Maslow's work has often been applied to the business world and is said to have influenced such notables as Peter Drucker. Specifically, the hierarchy of needs has been used to understand the motivation of employees.

We'd like to apply it in another direction, and that is the needs of your customers. The five basic needs Maslow identified are: physical, i.e., food and water; safety; a sense of belonging; esteem, and self-actualization, i.e., realizing one's potential. Does your product or service fit into this framework? Where? So critical is the customer relationship today that we must ask if we are meeting a genuine need, in which case the relationship has more chance of surviving, or just selling something, in which case customer whim can take over. Does your customer really need the 100th iteration of a brand of frozen pizza? Or is that just easy for you to do?

In this regard, it is interesting that in a speech a few years ago entitled, "The Innovation Imperative," GE CEO Jeffrey Immelt identified five keys to innovation. The first was people and processes.

> "The first thing is a clear mission. People need to know what their organization stands for and is trying to accomplish. So what does mission mean? Don't expect a 29-year-old engineer to embrace a financial objective as a statement of mission. People want to know what their organization is here for and how they can contribute."
>
> —Peter Drucker

If your products were removed from the market, would anyone miss them?

The second was, "placing the right bets." And he listed GE's bets: energy, health care, security, and the worldwide shortage of water. About as basic as it gets. GE bets big, and with great risk, on these needs.

The second concept is passion. Professor Yunus' passion for the poor in Bangladesh caused him to persevere until he found a solution. Passion—or call it persistence or drive or dedication—gets us past the difficulties of innovation. When companies like 3M, Gore and Google give their people free time to pursue their interests, they are creating an opening for individual passion to work.

Rethinking need and passion can take us to a deeper place in our work. This is not a feel-good illusion. Just the opposite, in fact. Making your numbers and looking just three months ahead is the illusion. Being passionate about meeting genuine needs is real. This is how Lord John Browne, CEO of British Petroleum, expressed it:

> "I believe that a good successful business is part of society, and exists to meet society's needs. That is the purpose of business at the highest level. We need to make money to reward those who have trusted us with their investment, but that isn't our primary purpose. We also need to behave responsibly, but I think that responsibility comes through what we do, and the way we do it—not by adding on some extra activity, or by adopting distracting concepts such as the triple bottom line. We are fulfilling our purpose by supplying goods and services, at a price people can afford, and in a manner which makes the activity sustainable."

In a turbulent world we need as many constants as we can create. Being passionate about meeting real needs strikes us as a trustworthy anchor.

The New Face of Government

Duck! Innovation, government style. Who really invented the Internet? A portal in 90 days? Google's secret. Better batteries. VCs come to Washington. Perfect storm, imperfect response.

I t's dusk. In full combat gear, and carrying our semi-automatic rifles, we are crawling through the dust beside a stonewall in a city that could be Baghdad. You are in the lead by about 10 feet. We know an enemy combatant is around the stonewall, somewhere in the shadows off to the right. You signal us to climb the wall to get to the flat roof of the adjacent building, and as we start to do so, gunfire erupts ...

For many soldiers in the U.S. Army, this is a realistic scenario. For us, however, it's virtual—we are players in an online video game created by the U.S. Army and distributed for free as a way to attract new recruits. Since its release in 2002, "America's Army" has attracted 7.5 million registered users, making it one of the most popular online games. Forty percent of new recruits say they have played the game. It has won more than 15 awards, such as the *Computer Gaming World* Editor's Choice award.

This is innovation, government-style. The game has inspired similar efforts in other branches of the military, and it is has been adapted as a training tool for the Army. For example, in real life the Army has moved the gunner atop a Humvee inside the vehicle so that he is less exposed to enemy shooters. The gunner will operate the gun from inside using video and other electronics—the experience is like playing a video game. So training on the America's Army game is perfect. This feature is being incorporated back into the game for non-military virtual gamers to experience.

"Some may knock the Army for this thinly veiled recruitment drive, but I'm going to salute—no pun intended. The Army is being up-front and honest about its intentions. Besides, video games really can be a good way to teach people."

—*Darren Gladstone*
Senior Editor
CNET Reviews

It is often thought that government can't innovate. Its bureaucracies are notoriously slow moving, there are no market incentives to innovate or perish, and turnover in the leadership ranks is so high that nothing that is enduring can be accomplished. There is truth in these beliefs, but consider just one thing: it was the U.S. government, through its Defense Advanced Research Projects Agency (DARPA), that invented the ARPANET, precursor to the Internet.

And that's only the tip of the iceberg. Starting in the 1960s, federal agencies like DARPA, including the National Science Foundation and the Office of Naval Research, poured tremendous sums every year into universities and corporations conducting research in computing and networking. Federal funding, for example, supported research into relational databases, theoretical computer science, artificial intelligence, and virtual reality, in addition to the Internet. It is hard to measure the results of this funding, but it is clear that the greatest digital innovations of our time owe much to government support. The technologies we take for granted everyday at work and at home might not exist, or might have been much slower in arriving, without this help.

Here's a little known fact: the two founders of Google, Larry Page and Sergei Brin, were graduate students in computer science at Stanford University. Stanford received funding from the Digital Libraries Initiative sponsored by several federal agencies, including the NSF and DARPA. Page was supported by the initiative as a graduate student researcher and Brin received an NSF fellowship. It was here that these two and others created the algorithm that is at the heart of the Google search engine.

The Nature of Innovation

So while we celebrate, justifiably, the accomplishments of these two digital pioneers and others such as Bill Gates and Steve Jobs, we must acknowledge the source of the money behind their work. From all of this emerge some interesting insights into how innovation works.

First, the digital revolution was the result of government, academia and corporations working together. Each had different needs and agendas at different times, but in their concerted efforts the field was kept moving forward. Government would pick up the slack when industry couldn't see the payoff. A National Research Council report put it this way:

> "Effective federal research has concentrated on work that industry has limited incentive to pursue: long-term, fundamental research; large system-building efforts that require the talents of diverse communities of scientists and engineers; and work that might displace existing, entrenched technologies. Furthermore, successful federal programs have tended to be organized in ways that accommodate the uncertainties in scientific and technological research."

As a metaphor for this type of collaboration, we might imagine three football players running down the field, tossing the ball off to one another as the situation requires. Again from the National Research Council Report:

> "The potential for unanticipated outcomes of research has two implications for federal policy. First, it suggests that measuring the results of federally funded research programs is extremely difficult. Projects that appear to have failed often make significant contributions to later technology development or achieve other objectives not originally envisioned.

> *"... IBM pioneered the concept of relational data-bases but did not commercialize the technology because of its perceived potential to compete with more-established IBM products. National Science Foundation (NSF)-sponsored research at UC-Berkeley allowed continued exploration of this concept and brought the technology to the point that it could be commercialized by several start-up companies—and more—established database companies (including IBM)."*

In all of this, we see the fits and starts of innovation, the collaboration of different parties with their different perspectives, the uncertainty of it all, and the need to let time sort things out. In a previous chapter we noted the criticism of Xerox for not commercially harvesting the fruits of its research lab. In this larger context, such criticism seems misplaced.

The DARPA Way

We have previously looked at corporate organizations designed to foster innovation. They actually have many common characteristics with DARPA. It is instructive to see how this nearly 50-year-old, enormously successful organization operates.

DARPA is small, with only 240 employees on the inside who enlist project team members on the outside. The organization is flat—only one layer of management between top and bottom. There is remarkable—for the government—freedom from bureaucratic control.

> "DARPA's only charter is radical innovation. We try to imagine what a military commander might want in the future and then change people's minds about what is technologically possible."
>
> —Anthony J. Tether
> Director, DARPA

TASK

Compare your organization's innovation strategy to DARPA.
What can you learn?

The technical staff is made up of world-class scientists and engineers from industry, universities and government labs—and they stay only three to five years, so that the agency is regularly reinvested with fresh thinking.

Everything at the agency is project-based. Projects typically last three to five years and are focused on end goals. They come to an end. The same area may be the target of a new project, but the decision to go ahead is a fresh decision.

Freewheeling thinking is encouraged, failure is not punished, and thinking big is the norm—but at the same time there is an emphasis on producing a result. Program managers are selected for their technical excellence, their entrepreneurial spirit and because they are "freewheeling zealots in pursuit of their goals." Because they are only around for four to six years, they feel free to change direction from their predecessors.

One other salient fact: with little overhead and no physical facilities such as labs, there is little institutional impediment to focusing purely on innovation. How often in corporations and other organizations do existing fiefdoms stifle any attempt to do something differently?

DARPA can be unconventional. In the past few years it has offered a $1 million prize to anyone who can build a fully autonomous, unmanned ground vehicle that could travel a significant distance at militarily relevant speeds, and hundreds of contestants have tried. Its most recent grand challenge: an autonomous vehicle that can resupply troops in an urban area. Top prize: $2 million.

DARPA officials meet regularly with military and civilian leaders in the Department of Defense to ask, "What keeps you up at night?" To these critical, near-term needs, DARPA then seeks to match solutions from its far-out research. The agency thus has its eyes on technologies of the future—what the next generation of commanders will need—but also its ear to the ground for solutions to current problems.

Let's recap and re-emphasize several important lessons. DARPA:

- listens to its "customers" for their critical needs, and these national defense needs are quite real. Recall the Grameen Bank's understanding of its customers' potentially life-changing needs.

- is open to ideas from anywhere. Compare its autonomous vehicle contest with Netflix' contest to improve its collaborative filtering software.

- collaborates with universities and corporations, just as social enterprises collaborate with governments and corporations.

- is a flat organization that has replaced top-down command and control with the granting of enormous responsibility to the people doing the actual work.

- has managed to combine anything-goes thinking with a process that drives its people toward results.

These organizational characteristics show up often enough in genuinely innovative organizations that we can safely recognize them as first principles of innovation.

What goes around comes around
One of the people to receive DARPA funding was Dr. Eric Brewer, a Professor of Computer Science at the University of California-Berkeley. Brewer created the search engine Inktomi based on his government-funded work and in 1966 created Inktomi Corp. to develop the search engine commercially. The search engine became one of the biggest in the market.

Meantime, in 1999, the federal government set about to build "FirstGov," a Web portal to more than 40 million government Web pages on more than 20,000 federal, state and local Web sites. Brewer donated his search engine to the effort, free for three years. President Bill Clinton decreed that FirstGov would be up and

> "FirstGov is an important step in making Government information and services available to the public 7 days a week, 24 hours a day. FirstGov—and electronic government, in general—offer the potential to revolutionize the way citizens and businesses interact with their Government. The benefits of this instant communication are plentiful, but the challenges are equally profound."
>
> — *U.S. Senator Steve Horn*

running in just three months—an almost impossible deadline in the government—but it was accomplished, in large part, because of Brewer's donation. FirstGov has received numerous awards for innovation.

Now, the Inktomi search engine was innovative, and a massive Web portal would have been considered innovative in 1999. But the real innovation of FirstGov was not the technology—it was the process through which FirstGov came into being.

Dr. Patricia Diamond Fletcher, Associate Professor in Policy Sciences at the University of Maryland-Baltimore County, teaches and conducts research on government information policy and system management. She and colleagues conducted a case study of FirstGov and came to some interesting conclusions about the success of the portal.

First off, the project was high on the agenda of President Clinton and had not only his full support but also his sense of urgency. The program stayed high on the presidential agenda when President George Bush took office.

QUESTION

Q

If you had to complete a major project in three months, how would you organize to do it?

Responsibility for the portal was given to the Government Services Administration (GSA). It set up a working group outside of the existing organization; the group had access to GSA resources but didn't have to follow standard operating procedures. "Thus," Fletcher writes in *Library Trends*, "team expertise and enthusiasm were not hampered by the red tape of bureaucracy."

The small size of the team enabled it to be flexible and to move quickly.

The team also enlisted the Federal CIO Council to be part of the project. These CIOs brought their professional expertise and knowledge of their agencies. Some 22 agencies actually contributed funding. Perhaps most important, however, the project now had their buy-in. "The agency CIOs were also co-opted to be change agents to convince agency personnel of the necessity of being a part of FirstGov," Fletcher writes.

In a previous chapter we discussed the nature of "need," and suggested that the greater the need being met, the greater the chances of success in an innovative venture. Everyone involved in building FirstGov, Fletcher says, considered it a necessary and important public service, the first step toward true e-government —they just knew "it was right."

We have also previously discussed the power of passion, and that seems to have played an important role here. The then CIO of the GSA was considered "an advocate, a proselytizer, and a very visible champion" for the project. Further, team members "expressed a sense of dedication to and belief in what they were doing."

Fletcher sums up this way:

> "This was not a typical government project, mired in procurement and acquisition regulations and constrained by the federal budget ... The FirstGov project was much more like that of a start-up "dot-com" fueled by the energy and engagement of its members and their belief in the project's goals and objectives.

> "Unlike most information technology projects in government, where procurement and acquisition law often contribute to lengthy, drawn-out, and costly information technology developments, FirstGov was not subject to many of these instances of red tape.

> *The requirement of a ninety-day project develop-*
> *ment meant that, to be successful, the team had to*
> *creatively, while legally, procure the necessary tech-*
> *nology to launch the portal on time. This created a*
> *sense of urgency that spurred the team to exceed*
> *their performance expectations."*

Are the lessons not obvious? If we translated this story to the corporate world, we would have a CEO committed and driven to create some new thing to meet a real need; vice presidents all signed on, even providing financial support; a small, tight-knit team operating outside bureaucratic procedures and passionately determined to succeed; and an atmosphere of urgency, creativity

TASK

Identify the rules, procedures, customs and organizational designs that impede innovation in your organization.

and enthusiasm. Does this sound like a dream? Well, it happened, right in the bowels of our greatest bureaucracy.

FirstGov hasn't sat still since its inception. It has been upgraded and given a new search engine. In 2005 it logged 179 million visits. Visitors applied for government jobs, sought student loans, and even bought stamps.

The Army and The VCs

Let's return to the U.S. Army for a look at another innovation. If you're old enough, you'll remember that VC once meant "Viet Cong." Today it means "Venture Capitalist."

As war has become ever more high-tech, the Army has had to become ever more creative in scouting and developing the technologies it needs. One solution is a venture capital fund, which invests in new technology companies. For example, as reported by *Federal Computer Week*, the $60 million fund has invested in a company called PowerPrecise Solutions, one of whose products is a battery charge indicator.

Soldiers need batteries for radios, shoulder-fired missiles and other tools. In 2004 the Army began noticing that its arsenals were running low on batteries. What it discovered was that soldiers going into battle were throwing out partially used batteries and replacing them with new ones—who wants to go into a fight not knowing how much life their batteries have?

PowerPrecise began delivering batteries with charge indicators—so that soldiers won't have to guess how much juice their batteries have left—several years ago, and they are expected to save the Army millions of dollars. At a ceremony in which the company presented the first such battery, Gary Davison, CEO of PowerPrecise, said, "What we are delivering today is the first battery, but what it really represents is what goes on behind the scenes."

The technology is cool, but the business model that made it a reality is hot.

Other federal agencies are using the VC approach. The first was the CIA, which invests in innovative companies through its VC arm known as In-Q-Tel. This firm, for example, invested in a company called Keyhole Corporation, which had created a 3-D earth-mapping program. The government got this technology and immediately deployed it in Iraq. Later, Keyhole was sold to Google, which offered the software to the public as Google Maps.

> "So look at our assumptions about technology or markets—suppose the opposite were true. Is there any evidence? Challenge your assumptions. This is basically looking at the vase upside down. Make yourself capable of doing this by building organized abandonment into your system. By asking yourself every few years, If we weren't doing what we now do, would we want to start doing it? And if the answer is 'probably not,' then maybe it isn't the right thing to do anymore. This is not very difficult. It's a habit more than a skill. But it's a habit you have to practice."
>
> —Peter Drucker

Identify how your organization reaches out beyond the walls to find the expertise and technology you need.

Since its launch in 1999, In-Q-Tel has:

- Delivered more than 130 technologies. These make it possible to fuse data from maps, images, text and other sources; visualize information in ways not previously possible; rapidly process vast amounts of information in multiple languages; make sense of seemingly unconnected information; and identify the most critical intelligence faster and more effectively.

- Engaged with more than 90 companies, most of which were previously unknown to the government, and more than 10 universities and research labs, which In-Q-Tel identified through its commercial and academic outreach programs and by reviewing more than 5,900 US and international companies' business plans.

- Cultivated a network of more than 200 venture capital firms, 100 labs and research organizations, further broadening the intelligence community's access to innovative technologies.

In a previous chapter we talked about the need for corporations to have their antennae out to discover what they don't know. The CIA has certainly done this, as one might expect from an intelligence agency. This is a fine example of networking, partnering and collaborating with other organizations to learn.

On the other hand

In the preceding examples of government innovation, what seems to be key is that the innovative activity took place outside of the normal processes of the bureaucracy. Back inside the walls, however, the story changes.

The federal government spends about $64 billion a year on information technology. In 2006 the Government Accountability Office (GAO) reported to Congress that of 857 major IT projects in the 2007 budget, 263—costing about $10 billion—had been identified as high risk, i.e., poorly planned or poorly performing.

One of these projects, Rescue 21, is a coastal communication system being developed by the Department of Homeland Security. The GAO reported:

> " ... *inadequacies in several areas contributed to Rescue 21 cost overruns and schedule delays. These inadequacies occurred in requirements management, project monitoring, risk management, contractor cost and schedule estimation and delivery, and executive level oversight. Accordingly, the estimated total acquisition cost has increased from $250 million in 1999 to $710.5 million in 2005, and the timeline for achieving full operating capability has been extended from 2006 to 2011.*"

Other well-known government technology flops include a new $2 billion IRS system and the $170 million FBI system for managing case files. The latter was scrapped before completion. Five CIOs and nine program managers watched that three-year train wreck happen. One of the government's big problems is that its CIOs have an average tenure of just 23 months. One reason is that they are paid less than they would be in the private sector. The CIOs acknowledge that a three to five year tenure would be best. How in the world can they get anything done in 23 months?

What went wrong with the FBI's Case File System project, which was begun in June 2001? Just about everything. When Robert Mueller was named FBI Director in September 2001, the agency didn't even have a CIO! Then it went through four CIOs before settling in 2004 on Zalmai Azmi, who had been with the Justice Department. Meantime, as work on the system continued, September 11 was forcing the agency to radically rethink its mission. An internal team was compiling requirements and an external team was building the custom technology. Everything was in flux, of course, and requirements kept changing. Meantime, off-the-shelf technology was advancing and becoming as good as what was being created. But this was a failure of management, not technology.

"In one division, I found we had 5 financial systems, 13 grant management systems, 6 acquisition systems, 6 personnel systems, and 13 separate e-mail systems. Now, how do you run a department like that?"

—*Tommy Thompson*
former Health and Human Services Secretary

The post-September 11 chaos in the agency reminds us of the "chaos" in the marketplace today—too many things changing too fast for the old ways of doing business.

CIO Azmi is addressing the agency's problems, moving to improve information sharing among the stovepipes, upgrading the IT infrastructure, and bringing IT into harmony with business processes. A new system called Sentinel, which replaces the Case File System, will lean more on Web-friendly, service-oriented technology than on customized solutions. Azmi has been given the kind of authority and budget control to do the job that many other government CIOs lack.

And, sadly, the FBI's technology woes, while well publicized, don't seem to be much different that any other agency's troubles. The government, through the GAO, has been trying to improve the management of technology, by giving CIOs real authority and influence and improving management processes generally, but the results are mixed. Consider: the CIO at the Department of Homeland Security isn't even listed among the 29 executives!

"Managing IT is big and complicated, and it seems to reflect all the complexities that the organization encounters in any of its other dimensions," Lester Diamond, then Assistant Director of the GAO, told us when he visited our offices in 2005. "When I see IT management fail in a broad way, I usually look to the organization. IT doesn't often fail by itself. I believe IT more often fails as a result of other organizational problems." Diamond was on a quest to learn about the CIO role in the corporate world so that the CIO role in government could be strengthened. We talked at length about what he had learned and what our research had revealed. It was clear in the exchange that government agencies needed a new management framework to make their deployment of technology both effective and efficient.

Perfect storm, imperfect response

Deficiencies become magnified in an emergency, and that was the case when Hurricane Katrina struck the Gulf Coast in 2005. It was the largest natural disaster in U.S. history, and lapses in the government's response can be understood. However, some things should simply not have happened. Federal and state computer systems tracking requests for supplies couldn't talk to each other, and the various systems within the DHS couldn't communicate. On the ground, first responders couldn't communicate, because their radios were not compatible. The National Guard relied on runners to stay in touch. The National Guard couldn't talk to the U.S. Army. Despite millions of federal dollars dedicated to communications, many local jurisdictions weren't prepared. One had given up satellite phone that might have given them some contact after the storm.

In matters of natural disaster and anti-terrorism we count on the government to get it right. We simply cannot tolerate business as usual. Diamond and his colleagues were trying to bring into government the best practices of technology management in the corporate world. We suggest that, as we've shown in this chapter, there are some best practices worth checking out within the government as well.

If FEMA didn't shine in its response to Katrina, one private individual did, demonstrating how innovative thinking can rise above chaos.

Parking lot innovation

In the parking lot of a Wal-Mart in hurricane-ravaged Chalmette, La., just outside of New Orleans, Dr. Enoch Choi examined a newly homeless woman who could remember only that she takes "blue pills." He pulled a microcomputer from his belt and wirelessly connected to a network created in just days by 150 corporations, nonprofits and government agencies. From it, Dr. Choi retrieved her prescription records and safely restored her medica-

> "The preparations for and response to Hurricane Katrina shows we are still an analog government in a digital age. We must recognize that we are woefully incapable of storing, moving and accessing information, especially in times of crisis."
>
> —*Select House Committee on Katrina*

tion. In this hot parking lot, hundreds of Katrina refugees began to see some order replacing the shattered circumstances of their lives.

It was not the technology Dr. Enoch Choi used so much, although that was critical, but how he managed it that mattered. He was sponsored by a Presbyterian church in California, worked under a tent erected by the National Guard, hooked into a prescription database through a cell wireless connection set up by Verizon, used five microcomputers he borrowed from OQO Inc., a new California company pioneering tiny computers, and treated up to 50 patients a day. He was passionate about his quest to solve a real human need, he reached out to organizations to get what he needed, and he just made it up as went along.

As he looked around, however, he saw no other such innovation. "FEMA," he said, "was using paper and pen."

Healer, Heal Thyself

Can you read Latin? Just one more form, please. 150 million phone calls. The computerized pizza parlor vs. the doctor's office. Coping during Katrina. Where's your medical history?

It's 3 p.m. on a Thursday. You've got a doctor's appointment in an hour; he wants to follow up on a cholesterol drug he prescribed. You turn to the screen on your desk and study the dashboard. All company systems in all regions are in the green zone. The logistics problem in Phoenix yesterday has been solved. No news on your competitors today. The system will shoot a note to your Blackberry if anything comes up. You email your wife about dinner and check your son's flight on your screen—he's coming home from college. Off you go.

At the doctor's office you approach the receptionist. She looks through a stack of manila folders and finds yours. She asks for your insurance card and makes a photocopy of it. You sit and thumb through a three-month-old news magazine. At 4:30 a nurse calls your name, and your 4:00 appointment begins. She weighs you and checks your blood pressure and writes some notes in your file.

At 4:50 the doctor enters the examining room, asks about the family, and opens your file. On top is a report that had been faxed over from a lab across town, but only after the nurse had asked you where the report was. You'd gone there last week to have blood drawn. You had shown your insurance card and handed the clerk a script specifying the tests your doctor wanted; it was a hand-written scrawl you couldn't decipher. "Is this for PSA?" the technician asked. No, you say, cholesterol. "Oh, yes, I see."

"Your numbers look good," the doctor says. He rifles through the file. "Are you taking any other medications?" Just the aspirin a day he had suggested, you reply. "How old are you?" he continues. "Have I sent you in to get your PSA test?"

You show the doctor an article you found on the Internet about the effect of grapefruit juice on cholesterol drugs. "I haven't seen this," he says, handing it back. You had this because you had set up your home page to collect news on cholesterol. You also use another site to shoot you emails with such news.

The doctor takes a small tablet and writes something in Latin. At the clerk station you hand over a $15 co-pay and as you wait for a receipt you look at the floor to ceiling shelves of manila folders. You gaze up at the smoke alarm on the ceiling.

Now you drive the little piece of paper your doctor gave you over to a pharmacy near your office—battling afternoon traffic for a half-hour. The GPS unit in your car alerts you to traffic snarls. At the pharmacy you trade the piece of paper for three months of pills, after once again showing your insurance card and then waiting another 25 minutes for the prescription to be filled. Finally, you are out of the pharmacy at 6:00 p.m., realizing you might not make it to the airport in time to pick your son up for his 7:00 p.m.

"Many physicians practice independently or in small groups, and ambulatory clinics, pharmacies, laboratories, rehabilitation clinics, and other organizations—although part of the delivery system—often act as independent entities. We often call this arrangement a "health care system," even though it was not created as a system and has never performed as a system."

—*National Academy of Engineering and Institute of Medicines*

"I recently had a surgical proce-
dure that is recommended for men
my age. I made my appointment
four weeks in advance, talked
with colleagues about what to
expect, followed the instructions
about what to eat and when, and
then went dutifully to my local
hospital, where I proceeded to
fill out my contact and insurance
information seven times. **Seven
times!** I cannot imagine doing
this in any other business, yet
we do it in healthcare without a
second thought. Just think of it:
seven different people will enter
my information into seven different and incompatible databases,
seven different times."

—*Mike Leavitt*
Secretary, Department of
Health and Human Services

arrival. Fact is, he will most likely need to take a taxi. You send him a text message, using your phone.

Now let's create one more scene, just to drive our message home. At 10:30 p.m. that night your son is watching a basketball game on TV, playing an online war game with participants all over the globe, sending instant messages to three friends, and purchasing movie tickets online.

As you prepare for bed, you suddenly feel weak and dizzy. You have a smashing headache. It is scary. Your spouse calls 911. Two emergency medical technicians who have never seen you in their lives show up, check your vitals and encourage you to go to the emergency room. There, sitting with a clerk, you fill out several forms and hand over your insurance card. You wait 56 minutes (the average in California). A nurse directs you to an examining area, checks your vitals again and writes on a paper chart. Eventually a resident, still in training, shows up, takes the chart, and asks, "Are you taking any medications?" You don't see a manila folder, but you suspect it's lurking somewhere.

Why do you put up with this?

You would long ago have cleaned up such an inefficient process in your company. Indeed, if your company insisted on operating this way, it would go under. You have brought technology into your professional and personal life to make you aware and efficient. And yet when it comes to your health, perhaps even your life, you must submit yourself to an antiquated and dangerous paper "system."

Oh, we are quite innovative when it comes to medical discoveries. American-born scientists working in the United States have won 12 Nobel Prizes in medicine over the past decade. Three more have gone to foreign-born scientists working in the United States. By comparison, researchers outside of the U.S. have earned just seven.

> "If we're going to meet the goal of improving the quality of care for all Americans, we have to be able to get to all the information about a patient, whether it's at a retail pharmacy, whether it's in another provider organization, whether it's in a payer organization, so that we can bring all the information related to a patient together at the right place, in front of the right person, so physicians and patients can make the best possible medical decision."
>
> —Dr. Martin Harris
> CIO, The Cleveland Clinic

But when it comes to using technology to build a business model for health care delivery, we are Luddites. In recent years U.S. health services have ranked 38th among 53 industries in business technology investment per worker. Health services spent less than one tenth what banks and other industries spent. That's why the afternoon visit to the doctor we imagined for you was so disjointed.

This is not about your inconvenience. Various studies have yielded this alarming picture:

- Every year medical errors cause 98,000 deaths (some studies suggest the number is twice that) and one million injuries. This is not a statistic. This is a national health emergency. And a scandal.

- Medical errors kill more people each year than breast cancer, AIDS, or motor vehicle accidents.

- Little more than half of patients receive the known best practices in care.

- Less than half of doctors in large practices provide the recommended care for patients with chronic diseases.

- Thirty to forty percent of the money we spend on health care —more than half a trillion dollars a year—is spent on costs associated with "overuse, under-use, misuse, duplication, system failures, unnecessary repetition, poor communication and inefficiency."

- One-fifth of medical errors are due to the lack of immediate access to patient information.

- Eighty percent of medical errors were initiated by miscommunication, including missed communication between physicians, misinformation in medical records, mishandling of patient requests and messages, inaccessible records, mislabeled specimens, mis-filed or missing charts, and inadequate reminder systems.

- Three out of every 10 tests are reordered because results cannot be found. Patient charts cannot be found on 30 percent of visits.

- As much as $300 billion is spent each year on health care that does not improve patient outcomes – treatment that is unnecessary, inappropriate, inefficient, or ineffective.

Why do we put up with this?

In previous chapters we have looked at technology-enabled business models in corporations, social enterprises and government. We have seen the need for leadership at the top and collaboration across silos and boundaries. We have talked about the need to get information flowing across these walls. And that's essentially what we are looking at here, except on a massive scale. We have a gaggle of players: doctors, hospitals, insurance companies, employers, government and researchers, all operating in an environment that just sort of happened.

"Any practicing physician can tell you a story about how missing information directly affected the care of one of his patients. Any medical practice administrator or hospital administrator can tell you about the large expense of tracking down missing inform ation. Illegible handwriting, confusing forms, lost paper work, misunderstood conversations in person or by phone, all clearly contribute to errors."

—*Dennis Shubert, M.D.*
Director, Maine Quality Forum

This "system" is usually analyzed by following the money. The explosion in medical knowledge over that past half century and the creation of new diagnostic and treatment procedures and equipment have sent the costs of medical heavenward, and the game has been shifting those costs around.

Patients whose care is paid for by employers or the government have no reason to not take advantage of it. Employers reduce benefits and raise premiums or drop medical insurance coverage altogether. Insurance companies hold doctors responsible for the amount of care they dispense and dispute more and more claims. Hospitals send patients home earlier than ever. Doctors spend less time with patients and worry if they order too many tests, because the insurance company will ding them, or order too few tests, opening them up to lawsuits.

Patients make endless calls to scream at insurance companies about denied claims. And on it goes.

Let's analyze the system from the perspective of information flows. Think about the model introduced earlier for corporations

QUESTION

Q

Do you store critical data about your customers in manila folders?

"We live in the Information Age, but our healthcare industry is stuck in the Stone Age."

—*Bill Frist*
Former Senate
Majority Leader

—the need for information to flow within the organization, to and from partners and from the external environment. Processes need to be established to enable collaboration. In the same way, a doctor needs information about a patient—current condition, medical history, information about the patient held by other doctors and institutions, and knowledge of the latest research and thinking about the condition affecting the patient.

The problem is that vital information is missing in one out of every seven primary care visits. Information is often unreliable—it's estimated that pharmacists make 150 million calls to doctors every year to clarify prescriptions; only about nine percent of U.S. doctors use an electronic system for prescriptions. What information is available must be transferred laboriously by paper; databases in hospitals and doctors' offices are often unable to talk to each other, because there are no data standards.

"Today in America, thousands of patients are having unnecessary tests, undergoing surgeries they do not need, and taking harmful drugs due to our paper-based health care system, and the consequences are deadly and costly. Because of this, sadly, hundreds of patients will die today and thousands more will be put at risk. And all of this can be prevented. Simply put, paper kills."

—*Congressman*
Tim Murphy

Does your company transmit vital, life or death information by handwritten, paper memos?

Creating all these silos of data is no small task: in some settings doctors and nurses spend as much time on paperwork as they do treating patients. Did you know that the 130,000 pages of Medicaid and Medicare rules and regulations are three times the size of the Internal Revenue code? Did you know that a Medicare patient arriving at the emergency room must sign eight different forms?

When all of this is resolved, and we think it will be eventually, the real innovation will not be the technology. It will be how the medical community rewires the way it works and collaborates. It's a people and organizational issue. We are accustomed today to seeing twice as many clerks as medical personnel in a doctor's office. That will change. There will be fewer visits to the doctor; information will be exchanged electronically. There will be fewer repeat tests. Doctors on rounds in a hospital will have everything they need to know in a small device hanging on their belts. Patients will have access to their medical records online, and so will the emergency room. But all this will require change, and change is not easy.

Actually, we already have the technology we need. A few examples:

"My pizza parlor is more thoroughly computerized than most of health care. It's high time to put the paper medical record where it belongs — in the Smithsonian, next to the typewriter."

—Dr. Donald Berwick
President of the
Institute for Healthcare

We have CPOEs, computerized physician order entry systems, with which doctors can file prescriptions and give orders for lab work. These can issue alerts on possible adverse drug interactions. Mistakes are reduced, as are time and costs.

We have EHRs, electronic health records, which capture every piece of information about a patient and are accessible to qualified medical personnel online. In an emergency the patient doesn't have to remember drugs he's taking and nobody has to track down a manila folder.

We have CDSS, clinical decision support systems. These advise doctors on the latest best practices in diagnosis and treatment, allowing them to customize what they do for an individual patient. This is controversial terrain. There is obviously a difference between what is known in the aggregate and what is right for an individual. And nobody wants insurance companies to use this information to turn doctors into robots; there is enough policing of physicians in the name of cost-containment today.

Nevertheless, when studies indicate that only about half of all patients get widely accepted and uncontroversial advice from their doctors – such as taking aspirin for heart conditions – it's time we considered something new. Moreover, if we had a national, inter-operative, medical information network, we would be able to see patterns in the aggregate data. We could learn, for example, whether a certain test is actually worthwhile in a certain situation. The quality of healthcare would go up and the cost would go down.

The Good News

Fortunately, major efforts are underway to make this kind of system a reality. The federal government has a plan to make electronic health records a reality for all within a decade. As part of this effort, the Department of Health and Human Services has been working with the private sector to establish data standards so that X-rays can be transmitted over the Internet, lab results can be sent electronically to the doctor, and prescriptions can be sent electronically to pharmacists. The administration is also pouring millions into grants to hospitals, doctors and others who are pioneering in health information technology.

> "Most industries in America have used information technology to make their businesses more cost-effective, more efficient and more productive, and the truth of the matter is, health care hasn't. Health care has been fantastic in terms of technological change. You see these machines in these hospitals—compared to what life was like ten years ago, things have changed dramatically. We've got fantastic new pharmaceuticals that help save lives, but we've got docs still writing records by hand. And most docs can't write very well ..."
>
> —*President George W. Bush*

Here is a sampling of innovative work in health care today.

The Veterans Health Administration Service is the largest integrated health system in the United States, with 5.3 million patients and 1,400 sites of care. Although it has not had a sterling reputation in the past, the VHA today is on the leading edge of innovation. It won the 2006 Innovations in American Government Award presented by The Ash Institute for Democratic Governance and Innovation at Harvard University's John F. Kennedy School of Government.

The VHA has created a system—Veterans Health Information Services and Technology Architecture (VistA)—that allows clinicians to view and edit electronic health records, and provides access to images such as x-rays, photos or documents, throughout its system. Veterans increasingly have access to their records and more opportunity to successfully manage their own health. The results are eye opening:

- VistA's computerized system checks for incompatible medications. While one in 20 outpatient prescriptions are complicated by medication errors nationwide, VHA's process fails at a rate of only seven per million.

- The use of clinical decision support and performance measurement to improve pneumonia vaccination rates helped save the lives of 6,000 veterans with emphysema. As VHA's vaccination rate became the national benchmark, pneumonia hospitalizations were halved even while VHA's patient population doubled—all while reducing taxpayer costs by $40 million.

- The President's Information Technology Advisory Committee (PITAC) estimates that nationally one in five lab tests are repeated because previous test results were not available at the point of care. The cost of maintaining VistA is $87 per patient per year, only slightly more than the cost of one unnecessarily repeated lab test.

- Adjusted for inflation, VHA care is 32% less expensive than a decade ago, although health care costs generally went up 50 percent. And the VHA has measurably better outcomes in quality, satisfaction, access and patient function. The VA outperforms all other sectors of American health care in of 294 measures of quality in disease prevention and treatment.

Wouldn't you like to be in that system?

We're all more aware of the threat of terrorist attacks and natural disasters. When hurricanes Katrina and Rita struck the Gulf Coast in 2005, the VA Medical Center in Gulfport, Mississippi, was destroyed, and the New Orleans VA Medical Center in New Orleans was evacuated and closed. Nevertheless, medical records for 40,000 veterans in the area were almost immediately available to doctors across the country, and veterans could resume their treatment and refill their prescriptions.

What is going on at VHA and at private clinics around the country will transform the practice of medicine. Business technology first brought efficiency and speed to corporations. Then it began to change the conduct of business. In the same way, technology has begun to improve the productivity of health care, but in the future it will bring hard to imagine changes in how we treat disease and keep people healthy.

The **Mayo Clinic** in Rochester, Minnesota, is one of the organizations at the forefront. Ironically, we might blame the clinic for the manila folder. Henry Plummer, the fourth physician at the clinic, which opened 100 years ago, pioneered the idea of having one record for each patient, which would travel with the patient, replacing ledgers and various notes written and kept by individual doctors in their offices. He also studied how industry moved information, and created a system of conveyors and pneumatic tubes to swish the records around the clinic.

This evolved into thick plastic jackets bulging with color-coded paper records. One patient might have as many as 40 of these jackets.

That's all gone now. The clinic has digitized 4.4 million patient records in a unified system. The system must handle 1.5 million outpatient visits and 60,000 hospital admissions each year. It is used by 15,000 caregivers and staff, who have access to 15,000 terminals across the Mayo campus. Every week, about 55,000 clinical notes are added to the system, and 125,000 outpatient orders are made electronically for diagnostic tests, medications or consultations.

This is the productivity phase, in which accuracy, speed and connectivity improve exponentially. Doctors on opposite sides of the campus can call up a patient's record on their screens and discuss it intelligently. Everything is in there—medications, history, even x-rays. This kind of technology is the norm in the corporate world.

> "Wouldn't it be marvelous if a doctor knew not just the exact location of the patient's cancer but its gene characteristics and the outcomes of therapy in the last 500 patients with cancer in that identical location and with those identical genetic characteristics? To do this, there needs to be a consistent way to link these kinds of data, not just in a single hospital, but regionally, nationally and globally."
>
> —*Hugh Smith, M.D.*
> *Vice President, Mayo Clinic*
> *Chair of the Board*
> *of Governors*
> *Mayo Clinic, Rochester*

Beyond this, however, lies the revolution. Using IBM's Blue Gene supercomputer, the clinic will mine all patient data, transcribed doctors' notes, outside databases, outside research and gene and protein knowledge to put right in front of the doctor everything that should be known about a patient. What has been learned from other patients and what is being discovered in the labs will be right there. You won't have to print out articles from the Internet and carry them to your doctor any longer! It can take 17 years for new research to make it into a doctor's office today. Not anymore.

Kaiser Permanente, the nation's largest HMO, which serves 8.2 million patients, is moving down a similar path. One of the new things these systems offer is the ability of the patient to see his or her own medical records, make appointments online, get reminders for drug refills and appointments, and see test results. This gives the patient more involvement in his or her own care and is likely to make them a better patient.

Dr. Robert Pearl is Executive Director and CEO of The Permanente Medical Group in Northern California. His advocacy of electronic medical records flows from personal experience. A few years ago his father, who lived half the year in New York and half in Florida, had his spleen removed. His doctors in both places were excellent. But each assumed the other had administered a post-operative vaccine that is common after these surgeries. One day at Dr. Pearl's home in California he found his father on the floor. He had succumbed to pneumococcal septicemia.

"He died because medical care has become incredibly complex and because as a nation we have not devoted enough attention to implementing electronic medical record systems and other methods to ensure patient safety," Dr. Pearl wrote.

His father, Dr. Pearl has said, kept track of the medications he was taking—on a worn piece of paper in his pocket.

Preparing for the Future

"It's tough to make predictions, especially about the future."
—*Yogi Berra*

Let's go back a decade to the blissful days of 1996 and try to remember how it was. Windows 97 was on the way, except it wasn't there quite yet, and it became Windows 98. It was Amazon's first full fiscal year. The Internet bubble was on its way, but, caught up in our irrational exuberance, we couldn't see it. Y2K was on the way, but not many of us were worried yet. Google? Not for another two years. Does our company need a Web page? Do you have an email address? Offshoring and globalization? What does all that mean?

In 1996 we were not able to foresee the world of 2006. The rise of China and India as economic powerhouses. The growth of open source software. The post-September 11 security issues. The crash and the need to cut costs. The siren call of outsourcing and off-shoring. And then the almost whiplash shift from bottom line cost cutting to top line revenue making. And, of course, the battle cry of "Innovation!"

If we couldn't foresee 2006, do you think we can grasp the world of 2016?

Some companies have hired futurists to try to make some sense of the future. One of them is BT Group, formerly British Telecom.

Every few years BT issues a "technology timeline," a look into the future at the technologies coming down the pike. Ian Pearson, a futurist employed by BT, gathers the information from many different sources. They are not hard and fast predictions, he says, just possibilities. We will cherry pick a few here to illustrate what the year 2016 might look like:

- Artificial intelligence (AI) teachers get better results than most human teachers
- AI entity earns college degree
- Computers that write most of their own software
- Human knowledge exceeded by machine knowledge
- AI member of parliament
- Academic learning is argued to be unnecessary in the age of smart machines
- Retirement age raised to 75
- Major pensions crisis
- More people using telework centres than home working
- Autonomous production plants make everything, Asia unemployment increases
- Retirement age linked to medical history
- Desktop computer as fast as human brain
- Bacterial supercomputer
- Reverse auctions in personal shopping devices (nearby stores bid to provide items on shopping list)
- Fully auto-piloted cars
- Hackers wipe out networks, causing chaos and mass starvation
- Computers and robots become superior to humans

Along with BT, we aren't saying these things will transpire. We just present this list to point out what some very serious, intelligent people are thinking about the future. This more or less random sampling of projections does prompt this thought, however:

technology will only burrow deeper into our personal lives and into our organizations, disrupting the way we do things and throwing more threats and opportunities in our way.

QUESTION

Does your organization have a formal process for assessing the future?

We will venture a few projections. As computing becomes more pervasive, it will become less visible. An example is "smart dust." These are tiny sensors that can be scattered around then report back to a network on the environment—noise, light, chemicals, vibration, temperature and the like. And on the horizon are RFID tags the size of pinheads that could be attached to any product as it makes its way through manufacturing and distribution. What this means is that we will be inundated by a new wave of information as the planet becomes increasingly connected. This wave of connectivity will be guided by four rules. Anything that can be digitized will be. Anything that can go wirelessly will. Anything that can get smaller will. And everything, seemingly, will want to be free.

Researchers at the Rand Corporation have peered ahead and come to some conclusions about the future. Technological changes will accelerate, they say, with implications for the way business is organized. Partly as the result of technology, globalization will continue apace and become even more expansive. Also as a result of the new technologies, organizations will continue to decentralize, leading to new kinds of relationships between employers and employees.

All of this, RAND says in a report entitled *The 21st Century at Work*, will cause us to train our future workers differently:

> "*The rapid pace of technological change is expected to continue to propel demand for highly skilled workers who can develop the new technologies and bring them to market and who can exploit the new technologies in the production of goods and services. ...*

In addition, technological developments, such as technology-mediated instruction, have the potential to improve educational outcomes and support lifelong learning through on-the-job training or training through other public and private institutions."

What this says to us is that organizations should be looking for employees who understand technology and can marry it to business strategy. It says to us, as well, that technology will move deeper into education, as it will in medicine and has in business, and that this will be necessary and good. A strategy for anticipating the future, we believe, must begin with the people who will be living it. If we prepare them well—and that will mean changes in what we are doing now—we will be preparing our organizations to deal with the unknowable.

On the surface higher education looks pretty much the way it did 200 years ago: ivy-covered, red brick buildings, the quad, the lecture hall. But in many places innovative applications of technology are abloom.

"Modern managers must develop a broad vision of the future and nourish organizational capabilities that will carry them forward successfully. This might be the ultimate managerial challenge.

"Research on the most successful firms and organizations over the past century reveals a timeless characteristic: respect for the value of human resources and skills and their continuing development. The most important strategy of all appears to lie in top management's appreciation of the people who build and sustain their enterprises, and in respect for their ability to learn and adapt to changing and challenging circumstances."

—*James Utterback*
Professor of Management and Innovation, MIT Sloan School of Management

How has your college or university changed since you graduated?

At Duke University and many other schools, for example, students and professors are using iPods for a lot more than downloading music. In 2004, Duke began giving iPods to its students for free. They use them to download lectures and to record information on field trips. Neurobiology students, for example, can download a multimedia glossary with more than 500 terms relating to the functional anatomy of the human brain. For each term, there is information on brain structure location and function, audio pronunciation, links to related terms and high quality brain images optimized for the iPod photo display. Other students carried their iPods on a service trip to the Gulf Coast after Hurricane Katrina. They used them to create audio journals and gave oral presentations when they returned, employing excerpts from interviews they conducted on the trip.

The iPod program has expanded across the campus, with hundreds of hours of lectures being recorded, including more than 700 in the medical school. Duke is deploying other new technologies, as well, including blog and wiki-like tools for online collaboration.

Schools are using other gadgets: tablet computers and even cell phones to connect teachers and students. You can, for instance, learn Chinese over your cell phone through a course offered by a non-profit organization called Connexions, which was started by a Rice University professor. Part of the course description:

> *"This course is presented in a moblog which is an effective medium for delivering small amounts of knowledge anytime, anywhere. It is also effective in drilling, which enables memorization. Furthermore, its ease of publication encourages users to interact. It can also bring together mentors, parents, adult and teenage learners to share their experience, ask ques-*

*tions, clarify doubts, and form bonds and friendship.
In this course, the core teaching materials and the
communication component are accessible via wireless
devices."*

The iPods, cell phones and other devices make programs such as this work, but the innovation—as we have written in other chapters about business, medicine and social enterprises—is in the new way of doing things. Notice the parallels in the transformation of these organizations. The people involved are scattered geographically, but the connections among them are stronger, and, in fact, collaboration becomes a key new element in the process, whether it's doing business, healing or teaching.

As in healthcare, examples of innovation can be found everywhere in education, and, similarly, we can glimpse a radical transformation somewhere down the road. Even with all the experiments in technology-enabled transformation, however, we still run our schools on the Agricultural Age calendar, giving the kids summers off so that they can "help on the farm." Except that they're not behind a plow; they're in front of TVs and computer monitors and video games, calling their friends on cell phones and sending instant messages, and Googling when they need to know something. Perhaps observing them awhile would be in order. They will be bringing these predilections into the workplace in a few years. Perhaps they are giving us an early warning of what is to come.

"The hurdles are built within the structure of a university, which is highly decentralized. Yet technology works best when it is holistic, linked, and networked. But that goes against the architecture upon which today's universities are built, which is very much silos and colleges and centers and fiefdoms."

—Marshall Goodman
VP and Campus Executive
Officer, University of South
Florida, Lakeland

> *If you have children, observe the way they use technology and find three things you might apply to your organization.*

We can see the seeds of transformation all about us.

Let's start with Connexions, which we mentioned earlier. This non-profit was launched in 1999 by Dr. Richard Baraniuk, an electrical and computer engineering professor at Rice University in Houston. It's a Web-based repository of college courses and textbooks. Professors can place their materials there and collaborate on them, and students can access them. The knowledge is created in modules, which can be collected into courses. Connexions now has 3611 modules and 190 courses in subjects ranging from computer science to music. Modules are available in Chinese, Italian, Japanese, Portuguese and Thai. More than one million people from 194 countries have visited the site.

> "People and their values shape technology, and can effectively delay or even prevent technological change. Today, strong social forces resist the introduction of various types of technology-enabled education. Most people usually oppose machines taking over their roles. Countless faculty members have a vested interest in prolonging face-to-face lecturing and discussion, printed textbooks, small classes and seminars, and individual, faculty designed syllabi. Faculty, in short, resist having their skills devalued."
>
> —*Thomas Hughes*
> *Professor Emeritus of the*
> *History of Science*
> *University of Pennsylvania*

The University of California at Merced is developing its intro-duction to biology and college algebra courses in Connexions. And electrical engineering faculty from Stanford, UC Berkeley, University of Illinois, Michigan, Wisconsin, Ohio State, Georgia Tech, Rice, Cambridge, and TU Norway are collaborating on a customizable digital signal-processing course.

The organization created XML-based, open-source content management software, but the real innovation is the new business model the software enables. Connexions believes that "knowl-edge should be free and open to use and re-use; that collaboration should be easier, not harder; that people should get credit and kudos for contributing to research and education; and that con-cepts and ideas are linked in unusual and surprising ways."

Moreover, it intends to:

> " ... disintermediate the academic publishing industry —allowing authors direct access to students. For example, a new 300 page, hard-bound engineering textbook sells for $15-$20, as opposed to $100-$150 from a traditional academic publisher. As a non-profit, we can be sustainable with this pricing structure. Our authors are typically motivated by academic rather than financial rewards. Since most academic authors make very little from the sales of their text-books and since Connexions offers much greater access to their materials, our model is very appealing to them."

We can add to this other academic digitation projects, as well as the efforts by Google, Amazon and Yahoo to digitize books. We can add Wikipedia, the global, collaborative encyclopedia, and its own Wikibooks project. The sum of all this would seem to be a global, free, instantly accessible library of knowledge and college of instruction. Will that be the case 10 years from now? What will it mean for us? Will we be any wiser or just inundated with data? How can we take advantage of this in the continuing education of our employees or in the daily conduct of our business? Can we take these emerging technologies and use them innovatively?

Let's go next to the University of Phoenix, which was launched in 1976 by Dr. John Sperling, a Cambridge-educated economist and something of a maverick. His insight was that traditional colleges and universities weren't designed for adults already in the workplace, who, for example, must pursue their education at night. Sperling's vision of a for-profit university catering to these students produced howls of protest from the educational establishment in California, where he was teaching at the time, and then again in Arizona, where he moved seeking a friendlier environment. Eventually he won accreditation.

Today the university has more than 190 campuses and learning centers in 41 states, Puerto Rico, Canada, the Netherlands, Mexico and on military bases across Europe. It also has an online "campus" and can blend the physical and virtual learning experience for its more than 200,000 students. The university has a faculty of more than 19,000, including more than 9,600 in the online campus.

Here is why we're highlighting Phoenix: the bulk of these faculty members are working in their fields—management, nursing, marketing and the like. They average 16 years of experience in the workplace. They are "first among equals" in the small groups of students where collaboration is key. If corporations can now go beyond their in-house gurus for "instruction" on their challenges, as we discussed in an earlier chapter, are we witnessing, given the University of Phoenix and Connexions and other such efforts, the educational equivalent of this? Does this mean that students will no longer be limited to the professors who happen to be on

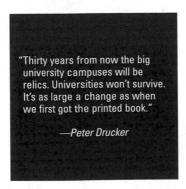

"Thirty years from now the big university campuses will be relics. Universities won't survive. It's as large a change as when we first got the printed book."

—Peter Drucker

the physical campus the student has chosen? Will these collaborative networks of students and teachers become as important as the collaborative networks corporations are building with their partners? Is the academy facing disintegration and decentralization in the same way corporations are?

Educational institutions that merely chase the technology risk getting sidetracked. All sorts of interactive software and "virtual reality rooms" are possible today, but they are expensive, and if they aren't conceived as part of a comprehensive educational "business plan," they will become costly diversions. These technological wonders are inventions, not innovations. As in a corporation, an educational invention becomes an innovation when it is brought into the marketplace to achieve a result.

QUESTION

If universities are disintegrated and decentralized, what happens to college football?

Next generation leaders

Aside from how it is trained, what is it that our next generation of leaders needs to know? If innovation is critical to navigating in a rapidly changing world, how do we prepare our navigators?

One thing we notice is that universities have been as siloed as corporations. By and large, you are a business management major or a computer science major, but not both. Each discipline has its own building, where its students take most of their courses and hang around with their own kind, and it would be odd if you ventured into another discipline's building. And when you graduate the whole job search process is equally siloed.

Analyzing trends in technology, the Rand Corporation sees a growing interaction among scientific disciplines, citing as an example materials scientists who increasingly work with computer scientists and application engineers to develop biomedical materials for artificial tissues. Each of these fields brings its unique approaches and views of the world. In *The Global Technology Revolution*, RAND sees these implications for education:

> "The multidisciplinary nature of technology is also changing the skills required by the workforce as well as R&D technologists. Developers increasingly need to understand vocabulary and fundamental concepts from other fields to work effectively in multidisciplinary teams, demanding more time in breadth courses. This trend may increase over time to the point where multidisciplinary degrees may be necessary, especially for visionaries and researchers who tie concepts together."

We will take this a step further to say that the convergence of business and technology management in the corporation, which we see as essential to innovation, will best be accomplished if it is begun in the university. Already this is happening.

At the University of Pennsylvania, some 200 students are enrolled in the Jerome Fisher Program in Management & Technology, a joint venture between the School of Engineering and the Wharton School of Business. It is dedicated to meeting the "growing need for people who can bridge the management and technical disciplines." Students earn two degrees, one in business and one in engineering. As Jerome Fisher, Founder and Chairman of the Nine West Group, said in endowing the program, "Understanding the relationship between business and technology is increasingly vital to building and maintaining competitive advantage in the global marketplace."

This interest is evident elsewhere. The Lally School of Management and Technology at Rennselaer Polytechnic Institute,

TASK

Identify the schools that offer cross-disciplinary training.
Are you recruiting there?

> "Keep an open mind about what you are studying and see how you can combine your interests. You'll see crossovers in business, technology and social issues... Figure out what you have a sincere interest in...and you should be able see business and technology impacting that subject. Think about what your end goal is —don't be afraid to challenge the status quo and go in your own direction."
>
> —*Eileen McCarthy*
> *2002 Graduate*
> *University of Pennsylvania*

for example, proclaims: "The conventional style of business education isolated from technology is obsolete ... the school's mission is to develop technically sophisticated business leaders who are prepared to guide their organizations in the integration of technology for new products, new businesses, and new systems."

If a graduate from one of these schools showed up to work at your company, would you know what to do with him? In what silo would you seat him?

In the early 20th Century corporations perfected the vertical organization with everything under one roof and held together by stovepipes. The academy dutifully supplied specialists for these pipes. Today the stovepipes are collapsing, a cross-disciplinary approach is imperative, and schools are responding. At Rennsalaer, for example, a newly-revised MBA curriculum is built around five courses: creating and managing an enterprise; networks, innovation, and value creation; developing innovative new products and services; formulating and implementing a competitive business strategy; and managing the business implications of emerging technologies.

We can't predict the future. But we can make sure the next generation of leaders is prepared to live it, make sense of it and orchestrate its ever-moving parts to our advantage.

Holistic Imagination

Journalists are taught that every story should answer who, what, where, when, how and why. We'll borrow this formulation to frame our advice on an innovation strategy, one that can guide us in a global, high-speed, frantic, Darwinian world.

We will assign to you as a leader two of the questions. The first is "why?" It should be your daily mantra. Why are we in business? Why do we do things the way we do? Why is it working? Why is it not working? Why should I be worried? Why not try this? Why do we believe what we believe? The answer will come back, "Because …" And to that you ask why again, slowly peeling back the onion of unexamined assumptions and comfortable routines.

Isn't this a critical challenge for all of us, even in successful companies? As we have written, innovation is first a mindset. Irving Wladawsky-Berger, Vice President for Technical Strategy and Innovation at IBM, is the author of a blog on innovation. In one entry, he describes the danger IBM faced in the early 90s. "The reason we got into so much trouble to begin with," he says, "is that while the marketplace was changing all around us, we did not like the changes and were slow to embrace them. We liked things as they were."

IBM was able to pull itself out of that valley of death because it stopped accepting "because" as the final answer. More than a decade after the death bell sounded, IBM is thriving, changing, trying new things—an elephant dancing, to borrow from the title of Lou Gerstner's book. Is it an innovative company? It's No. 10 on a list of the most innovative companies compiled by BusinessWeek and the Boston Consulting Group, which surveyed more than 1,000 executives worldwide for their opinions. A more telling metric, however, is that IBM is still with us. Surviving is the new metric of success.

In the No. 5 spot in that survey is Microsoft. Microsoft, of course, is the company everyone loves to hate. Its critics are vociferous in describing it as the "anti-innovation" company. We would just say that its original vision of "a computer on every desk" has come true, powered by Microsoft. For good or ill, it has created a standard for desktop applications that allows communication across boundaries. If it didn't invent all the technologies beneath its products, as critics correctly note, it did make them commercial realities. An invention becomes an innovation only when it finds profitable life in the marketplace. James Watt didn't invent the steam engine—he improved it and made it a practical tool in industry.

The second question we would assign to you as a leader is "who?" Who will take your organization into the 21st Century? Who among your current staff has the attitude? Whom will you hire? Answer those questions correctly and you can turn the what, when, where and how over to them to answer.

That seems to be Microsoft's plan. Just as the world shifted on IBM, it is now shifting on Microsoft, away from proprietary desktop software to open source and Web-based. At the same time, as Bill Gates plans to step away from day to day activity, the company is bringing up a new generation of leaders. One of them is J Allard, Vice President for design and development in the entertainment and devices unit. He led the development of Microsoft's Zune music player. "The only way to change the world is to imagine it different than the way it is today," he says. "Apply too much of the wisdom and knowledge that got us here, and you end up right where you started. Take a fresh look from a new perspective, and get a new result."

Companies do thrive in this difficult world. GE, 3M, UPS, FedEx, Wal-Mart reinvent themselves as necessary. Innovation is different in each—sometimes product, sometimes process, sometimes business model. They don't fixate on one solution, don't allow themselves to get trapped in a tunnel vision. They have a holistic imagination: what will we have to do to be in business a year from now, five years from now, ten? And then they do it.

This is sustained innovation. We can see it in all organizations. Professor Yunus' Grameen Bank has been experimenting and innovating for three decades, throwing off all kinds of new ideas. We see it even in government. I [Faisal Hoque] was invited by Mohamed Maghlaoui, the Algerian minister of transportation, to advise on a transformation effort. The transportation ministry was seeking to spin off its separate parts—its airline and train system, for example—but retain a shared infrastructure and shared services organization to support each. How do you transition to this new business model? How do you nurture this innovation and make it a reality?

Successful organizations are guided by several principles:

Convergence of disciplines and silos lets them act as one. Especially convergence in the management of business and technology; business ideas cannot be separated from the engine of execution.

Collaboration, enabled by business technology, is a common characteristic across all innovative companies—collaboration across internal and external boundaries.

Organizational design is critical to realizing convergence and collaboration.

Partners and networks provide ideas and capabilities the organization lacks. Most smart people work somewhere else.

Customers have ideas, too, and they aren't theoretical or wishful thinking. Customers are the ultimate reality check.

What these principles have in common is that they are about bringing people together. The positive stories we've related in this book all involve bringing people together in one way or another.

And behind the negative stories we usually find that people are not communicating, understanding each other, working together. Today, with the Internet and other technologies, people are coming together in ways unimaginable not long ago. One expression of this is the rise of social networks, virtual connections of people with social or professional interests. Innovative ideas once exchanged in meetings or at conferences can now be shared at the speed of light among infinitely more people anywhere.

None of these connections will lead to much, however, with imagination. After September 11, 2001, the phrase "failure of imagination" came into vogue and has been applied to events in many areas. It may seem obvious to say that organizations falter because of a lack of imagination, but if it's obvious why do they continue to stumble? We are awash in information, we know so much, and yet ...

On the wall in the conference room where we have worked on this book is a photo of Albert Einstein with his wild shock of hair and these words from him: "Imagination is more important than knowledge."

Faisal Hoque
Chairman and CEO, BTM Corporation
Author, *e-Enterprise*, *The Alignment Effect*, *Winning The 3-Legged Race*, and *Six Billion Minds*

Faisal Hoque is the Founder, Chairman and CEO of the Business Technology Management Corporation (BTM Corporation), which leads the industry in the convergence of business and technology with its solutions, research, platforms, and management services. He is the author of *The Alignment Effect* (Financial Times/Prentice Hall, 2002), *Winning the 3-Legged Race* (BTM Institute/Financial Times/Prentice Hall, 2005), and *Six Billion Minds* (BTM Institute/Aspatore, 2006), among other publications. A former senior executive at General Electric (GE) and other multinational corporations, Mr. Hoque is an internationally known visionary entrepreneur, innovator, and award winning thought leader. He conceived and developed Business Technology Management (BTM) to help organizations build better enterprises by managing business and technology together. He has written numerous articles for such publications as *BusinessWeek*, *The Economist* and *The Wall Street Journal* and is a sought-after public speaker.

Mr. Hoque founded BTM Corporation in 1999. He created its unique business model—a one-stop solution for BTM with a holistic management framework, software applications, management templates, research, knowledge, and a global expert network for managing business and technology together in the world's leading corporations, governments, and not-for-profit organizations. BTM Corporation has experienced record growth since its inception. The wingspan of BTM Corporation's success now exceeds 12 major industries, including manufacturing, consumer goods, hospitality, financial services, insurance, defense, government agencies, and utilities.

Mr. Hoque's multi-faceted expertise comes from nearly two decades of hands-on experience helping an array of leading private and public sector organizations to create and manage business innovation from their technology investments. He has guided the likes of American Express, Chase, CompUSA, Dun and Bradstreet, General Electric, Great American Insurance, JP Morgan, MasterCard, Pitney Bowes, PACCAR, and PepsiCo, among others. Through this perspective he has ushered his groundbreaking vision for the industry's first management science of business technology management to the forefront. He introduced this concept in his book *The Alignment Effect*.

The book was the catalyst for Mr. Hoque to launch several cross-disciplinary research and educational initiatives with global support from academic, industry, and thought leadership communities to bridge the gap between business and technology. An entrepreneur and innovator at heart, Mr. Hoque built his first commercial business technology product at the age of 19 while studying at the University of Minnesota. He founded two other award-winning companies prior to the BTM Corporation and has personally led over $200M in private equity and venture capital transactions for various early-to-growth stage companies. Mr. Hoque began his career with management positions at Dun & Bradstreet and Pitney Bowes. In 1994, GE Capital recruited Mr.

Hoque, then one of its youngest technology executives, to launch a comprehensive B2B electronic commerce spin-off.

Mr. Hoque is passionately committed to raising awareness of social, economic, and global cultural issues and actively works to promote non-violence and economic development for the under-privileged. He serves on several international boards of directors and/or advisory boards of global organizations addressing these issues with Nobel Laureates, accomplished business and industry leaders, leading academics, and prominent government officials around the globe.

For more information on Faisal Hoque, please visit: www.faisalhoque.com

Terry A. Kirkpatrick
Editor-in-Chief, BTM Corporation
Editor and Contributor, *Winning The 3-Legged Race* and
Six Billion Minds

Terry A. Kirkpatrick, Editor-in-Chief of the BTM Corporation, is responsible for its publication program, which includes management papers, books and magazine articles. He was the editor and a contributor to *Winning The 3-Legged Race* and *Six Billion Minds*, the BTM Press' most recent books.

He has extensive experience as a writer and editor at leading business technology magazines and knowledge-driven enterprises. He has been a Contributing Editor of Booz Allen Hamilton's *strategy+business* management journal, where he wrote about organizational design and change management. As a Contributing and Deputy Editor of *CIO Insight* magazine, he produced significant stories on a range of business and technology issues. He has also written and edited for McKinsey & Co. and Gartner, Inc.

Mr. Kirkpatrick was Editorial Director at the Peppers and Rogers Group, a customer relationship management consultancy, where he launched *1to1 Quarterly*, a thought leadership journal, and managed a portfolio of magazines and newsletters. Previously, at IBM, he launched the award-winning *Think Leadership* website for chief executive officers. He also launched an internal site for the company's scientists and technicians.

He was a managing editor of *The Reader's Digest* prior to that, responsible for the creation of the U.S. edition's monthly issues. He began his career at The Associated Press, where he was a national business and feature writer. His stories on a variety of subjects, including demographics, economics, energy, education, and the securities markets, were featured in newspapers and their magazine supplements across the country and around the world. He holds a master's degree in journalism from Louisiana State University and a bachelor's degree in economics from Louisiana Tech University.

REFERENCES

Chapter 1

Berner, Robert, "Why P&G's Smile Is So Bright," *BusinessWeek Online*, August 1, 2002.

Blass, Eileen, "GE always has innovation on its mind," *USA Today*, November 10, 2002.

Burrows, Peter, "Apple's Blueprint for Genius," *BusinessWeek Online*, March 21, 2005.

Efrati, Amir, "The Internet-Age Garage Sale," *The Wall Street Journal*, April 22, 2006.

Hansson, Magnus, "Sony Ericsson's Profit Soars, Boosted by Walkman Phones," *The Wall Street Journal*, April 13, 2006.

Hesseldahl, Arik, "Dell's High-End Home Run," *BusinessWeek Online*, February 17, 2006.

Hof, Robert D., "At P&G, It's '360-Degree Innovation,'" *BusinessWeek Online*, October 11, 2004.

Johnston, Martin, "SpinBrush creator comes clean," *Wharton Journal*, October 6, 2003.

Kroll, Luisa, "A Fresh Face," *Forbes.com*, July 8, 2002.

Lefkow, Dave, "The Talent Story of the iPod," Electronic Recruiting Exchange, December 1, 2005.

Shachtman, Noah, "The Federal Bureau of Luddites," *Slate*, April 4, 2006.

"Toys and Spinning Brushes: How John Osher Found His Way to Profits," *Knowledge@Wharton*, November 19, 2003.

Chapter 2

Carreyrou, John and Martinez, Barbara, "Research Chief Stirs Up Merck By Seeking Aid From Outsiders," *The Wall Street Journal*, June 7, 2006.

Drucker, Peter F., "The Next Information Revolution," *Forbes ASAP*, August 24, 1998.

Gerstner, Louis V. Jr., *Who Says Elephants Can't Dance? Inside IBM's Historic Turnaround*, HarperCollins Publishers Inc., 2002.

"Of Surgery and Symphonies, or the Well-Tempered Clavicle," *Toledo Alumni Magazine*, Fall 2003.

"Microsoft's Multiple Challenges: Is Its Size a Benefit or Burden?" *Knowledge@Wharton*, May 17, 2006.

Rudy, Lisa Jo, "Man of Action," *Penn Arts & Sciences Newsletter*, July 13, 2004.

Schneidman, Diane, "Renaissance man endows award for surgical investigators," *Bulletin of the American College of Surgeons*," May, 2005.

"SOM Alumnus Endows Professorship, Online Meetings in Vascular Surgery," *The Gazette Online*, The Newspaper of the Johns Hopkins University, Vol. 32, No. 33, May 5, 2003.

Useem, Michael, "Tip of the Spear: Leadership Lessons from the U.S.-led Armed Forces in the Middle East," *Knowledge@Wharton*, May 17, 2006.

Chapter 3

Brown, John Seely and Duguid, Paul, "Creativity Versus Structure: A Useful Tension," *MIT Sloan Management Review*, Summer, 2001.

Carey, David, "In conversation: an exclusive interview with FedEx CIO Robert Carter," *CIO Canada*, October 1, 2004.

Charan, Ram, *Profitable Growth is Everyone's Business*, Crown Business, 2004.

Dell, Michael, *Direct From Dell, Strategies that Revolutionized an Industry*, Harper Business, 1999.

"Expanding the Innovation Horizon, The Global CEO Study 2006," IBM, 2006.

Hoque, Faisal, et al, *Winning the 3-Legged Race: When Business and Technology Run Together*, Prentice Hall, 2006.

"How Does Your Knowledge Flow? An Interview with John Seely Brown," *CSC World*, December 2004 – February 2005.

"Innovation 2005," The Boston Consulting Group, 2005.

Jaruzelski, Barry, Dehoff, Kevin and Bordia, Rakesh, "Money Isn't Everything," *strategy+business*, Winter 2005.

Light, Geoff, "CRM Technology Enables One-to-One Customer Relationships," *DM Review*, August 2005.

"Majority of companies worldwide not equipped to achieve in new year," Bain & Company press release, February 3, 2006.

Scanlon, John, "Capital One Exec Addresses Alignment," *CIO Insight*, January 8, 2003.

Chapter 4

Anderson, Howard, "Why Big Companies Can't Invent," *Technology Review*, May 2004.

Arnold, David, "Observe. Learn. Invent," *The Boston Globe*, April 7, 2005.

Barnes, David, "How Business Should Drive Technology," *Optimize*, April 2006.

Bulkeley, William, "Got a Better Letter Opener?" *The Wall Street Journal*, July 13, 2006.

Chen, Kathy and Dean, Jason, "Low Costs, Plentiful Talent Make China a Global Magnet for R&D," *The Wall Street Journal*, March 13, 2006.

Chesbrough, Henry, "Reinventing R&D Through Open Innovation," *strategy+business* enews, April 30, 2003.

Clark, Hannah, "Can You Outsource Innovation?" *Forbes*, August 24, 2006.

Cone, Edward, "Boeing: New Jet, New Way of Doing Business," *CIO Insight*, March 6, 2006.

Delaney, Kevin, "Hope to Overtake Its Rivals, Yahoo Stocks Up on Academics," *The Wall Street Journal*, August 25, 2006.

Deutschman, Alan, "The Fabric of Creativity," *Fast Company*, December, 2004.

Engardio, Pete and Einhorn, Bruce, "Outsourcing Innovation," *BusinessWeek*, March 21, 2005.

Glass, David and Gilman, Hank, "The Most Underrated CEO Ever," *CNNMoney.com*, April 5, 2004.

Greenemeier, Larry, "On The Line At UPS," *InformationWeek*, January 23, 2006.

Grice, Corey, "Iridium asks court to let satellites burn," *News.com*, January 2, 2002.

Haddad, Charles, "UPS vs. FedEx: Ground Wars," *BusinessWeek*, May 21, 2001.

Hagel, John and Brown, John Seely, "The Shifting Industrial Landscape," *Optimize*, April 2005.

Hamel, Gary, "Management ala Google," *The Wall Street Journal*, April 26, 2006.

Hamm, Steve, "Adding Customers to the Design Team," *BusinessWeek*, March 1, 2004.

Lilien, Gary, Morrison, Pamela, Searls, Kathleen, Sonnack, Mary, and Von Hippel, Eric, "Performance Assessment of the Lead User Idea Generation Process for New Product Development," MIT Sloan School of Management Working Paper # 4151, January, 2001.

Iansiti, Marco, Favaloro, George, Utzschneider, James, and Richards, Greg, "Why IT Matters in Midsized Firms," Harvard Business School Working Paper Series, No. 06-013, September 1, 2005.

Lawton, Christopher, "Consumer Demand and Growth In Laptops Leave Dell Behind," *The Wall Street Journal*, August 30, 2006.

Marquardt, Michael, *Leading with Questions: How Leaders Find the Right Solutions By Knowing What To Ask*, Jossey-Bass, August 2005.

McGregor, Jena, "How Failure Breeds Success," *BusinessWeek*, July 10, 2006.

Palmer, Andrew, et al, "Foresight 2020 Economic, industry and corporate trends," Economist Intelligence Unit, 2006.

Taylor, William, "Get Out of That Rut and Into the Shower," *The New York Times*, August 13, 2006.

"The Rise of the Creative Consumer," *The Economist*, March 10, 2005.

Schwartz, Evan, "What Steve Wozniak Learned from Failure," *Working Knowledge*, Harvard Business School, September 13, 2004.

Seil, Bill, "How the right tools and an inclusive culture support the 787's global partner network," *Boeing Frontiers*, August 2006.

Von Hippel, Eric, "Companies Look for Ideas in All the Wrong Places," *CIO Insight*, June 5, 2005.

Von Hippel, Eric and Sonnack, Mary, "Breakthroughs to Order at 3M," MIT-Sloan School of Management Working Paper, January, 1999.

Chapter 5

Bellman, Eric, "Entrepreneur Gets Big Banks To Back Very Small Loans," *The Wall Street Journal*, May 15, 2006.

Brooke, James, "Rural Cambodia, Though Far Off the Grid, Is Finding Its Way Online," *The New York Times*, January 26, 2004.

Chon, Gina, "Bernard Krisher: Healing the Killing Fields," *Asiaweek*, June 29, 2001.

Clark, Don, "Intel Aims to Bridge Digital Divide," *The Wall Street Journal*, May 2, 2006.

Gangemi, Jeffrey, "Muhammad Yunus: Microcredit Missionary," *BusinessWeek*, December 26, 2005.

"Launching of Grameen Danone Foods Social Business Enterprise," Groupe Danone press release, March 16, 2006.

Markoff, John, "Intel to Offer Its Own Plan for Global Internet Access," *The New York Times*, May 2, 2006.

Miller, Jeff, "The village people," Mass High Tech: *The Journal of New England Technology*, December 10, 2004.

Yunus, Muhammad, Statement before the ITU World Information Award Ceremony, May 17, 2006.

Chapter 6

Chabrow, Eric, "State Of The Union," *InformationWeek*, November 28, 2005.

Dobson, Jason, "Army Game Project's Frank Blackwell on America's Army," *Serious Games Source*, 2006.

Fletcher, Patricia, "Creating the front door to government: a case study of the Firstgov portal," *Library Trends*, Fall 2003.

Funding a Revolution: Continuing Support for Computing Research, National Academy Press, 1999.

Greenemeier, Larry, "Tech vs. Terrorism," *InformationWeek*, June 6, 2005.

Jonsson, Patrik, "Enjoy the video game? Then join the Army," *The Christian Science Monitor*, September 19, 2006.

Kane, Pat, "Toy Soldiers," *The Guardian*, December 1, 2005.

Keizer, Gregg, "IRS Gives Away $318 Million Because Of Bungled Software Upgrade," *InformationWeek*, September 5, 2006.

Kolodney, Steve, "Lessons from the Front Lines of E-Government," *Public CIO*, May 17, 2006.

"The Federal Bureau of Investigation's Management of the Trilogy Information Technology Management Project," Audit Report 05-07, Office of the Inspector General, February 2005.

"The Shape of Things to Come: An Interview with Peter F. Drucker," *Leader to Leader*, Summer 1996.

Vizard, Frank, "High-Tech Video Game Trains Soldiers," *Popular Mechanics*, June 2005.

Chapter 7

"A Healthy System," Technology CEO Council, 2006.

Berwick, Donald, "How To Fix The System," *Time*, May 1, 2006

Daniel, Jodi, "Federal Health Information Technology Initiatives," Office of the National Coordinator for Health IT, May 5, 2006.

Finerfrock, Bill, "Presentation on Electronic Medical Records in Rural Health Clinics," Teleconference, Health Resources and Services Administration, 2005.

Fonkych, Kateryna and Taylor, Robert, "The State and Pattern of Health Information Technology Adoption," Rand Corporation, 2005.

Gibbs, Nancy and Bower, Amanda, "Q: What Scares Doctors? A: Being the Patient," *Time*, May 1, 2006.

"Going Digital: The Paper Trail Stops," Mayo Clinic, Friday, July 16, 2004.

McGee, Marianne, "Custom Care," *InformationWeek*, October 18, 2004.

"Mayo Clinic, IBM Aim to Drive Medical Breakthroughs," Mayo Clinic press release, August 04, 2004.

McGrath, Dylan, "Commentary: The sorry state of U.S. health care IT," *EE Times*, March 7, 2006.

McKaughan, Jeff, "Interview with Carl E. Hendricks," *Military Medical Technology*, May 08, 2006.

"National Center for Health Statistics: Preliminary Data for 1998 and 1999," Institute of Medicine and Centers for Disease Control and Prevention, 2000.

Pulley, John, "Health IT struggles echo 19th century challenges," *Government Health IT*, June 2, 2006.

"Reactive to Adaptive: Transforming Hospitals with Digital Technology," Health Research Institute & Global Technology Center, PriceWaterhouseCoopers, 2005.

Reid, Proctor, Compton, W. Dale, Grossman, Jerome, Fanjian, and Fanjiang, Gary, "Building a Better Delivery System: A New Engineering/ Health Care Partnership," National Academy of Engineering and Institute of Medicine, The National Academies Press, 2005.

Rothfeder, Jeffrey, "Can IT Save the Healthcare Industry?" *PC Magazine*, November 1, 2004.

Smith, Peter, et al, "Missing Clinical Information During Primary Care Visits," *The Journal of the American Medical Association*, February 2005.

"Transforming Health Care: The President's Health Information Technology Plan," www.whitehouse.gov.

Wallace, Scott, "Ending the Document Game: Connecting and Transforming Your Health Care Through Information Technology," Commission on Systemic Interoperability, 2005.

Waller, Douglas, "How VA Hospitals Became The Best," *Time*, September 4, 2006.

Chapter 8

Anton, Philip, Silberglitt, Richard and Schneider, James, "The Global Technology Revolution: Bio/Nano/Materials Trends and Their Synergies with Information Technology by 2015," Rand Corporation, 2001.

Blaisdell, Mikael, "Academic MP3s : Is It iTime Yet?" *Campus Technology*, March 2006.

Davies, Laurie, "Meet John Sperling, the man who revolutionized higher education in America," *Future*, University of Phoenix, Spring, 2006.

Drucker, Peter, "Seeing things as they really are," *Forbes*, March 10, 1997.

Earp, Samantha and Belanger, Yvonne, "End of Year Report on the 2005-06 Duke Digital Initiative," Duke University, July 24, 2006.

Frey, Christine and Cook, John, "How Amazon.com survived, thrived and turned a profit," *Seattle Post-Intelligencer*, January 28, 2004.

Karoly, Lynn and Panis, Constantijn, "The 21st Century at Work: Forces Shaping the Future Workforce and Workplace in the United States," Rand Corporation, 2004.

Mills, Elinor, "Yahoo to digitize public domain books," c/Net www.news.com, October 3, 2005.

Utterback, James, "The Dynamics of Innovation," from *The Internet and the University: Forum 2002*, EDUCAUSE and the Forum for the Future of Higher Education, 2003.

Voyles, Bennett, "IT Leadership: CAO 2.0," *Campus Technology*, November 2006.

Conclusion

Wladawsky-Berger, Irving, "Survival as the Mother of Invention," Irvign Wladawsky-Berger blog, September 11, 2006.

Greene, Jay, "The Soul of a New Microsoft," *BusinessWeek*, December 4, 2006.

INDEX

The Alignment Effect
How to Get Real Business Value Out of Technology

WHY aren't we getting real business value out of technology? One thing is sure: companies that continue to repeat the mistakes of the past will never reap the rewards of the future.

Most companies fail to capitalize on the technologies they already have; and many more are poised to meet this same fate with the next big technology fad spawned in Silicon Valley and propelled by venture capitalists. Whether it's wireless, Web services, or the latest and greatest in nanotechnology, companies will never get value-real or perceived-without first solving the business/technology disconnect.

The cataclysmic end of the new economy signaled not only a stock market implosion, but also a dramatic denouement in what was actually a decade-long history of "technology for the sake of technology." In retrospect, this revelation and return to rational thinking seem self-evident: what executive, after all, would willingly throw millions of dollars at an investment without knowing how it could affect their business? If we use history as a guide and tally up the waste, the answer is an unpalatable "a lot."

But now, corporations are demanding the same accountability from their IT investments that they do from their other assets, as they hold technology initiatives to real, bottom-line business results. As any decision-maker charged with overseeing how technology affects the business and vice versa knows, get it right and you're lionized as a savior; get it wrong and you're cast out as a pariah.

In *The Alignment Effect*, Faisal Hoque combines proven guidance with object lessons from Fortune 500 executives and industry authorities to compellingly illustrate how corporations can align themselves through Business Technology Management, thereby increasing their efficiency and reducing the financial and operational risks that have long been associated with business and technology change.

For information on this book please visit:
www.btminstitute.org/TheAlignmentEffect/

" *The Alignment Effect paints a vivid picture of information technology's worst-kept secret: IT cannot, by itself, solve your business problem. To solve your problem, any new technology must be carefully aligned with your business objectives and processes. Otherwise, save your money. Read this book if you want to ensure the success of your own technology implementation!*"

— *Don Peppers and Martha Rogers, Ph.D.*
Best-selling authors of the One to One series of books

About the Author

Faisal Hoque

Chairman and CEO, BTM Corporation

Author of *e-Enterprise, The Alignment Effect*, *Winning The 3-Legged Race, Six Billion Minds* and *Sustained Innovation*

Winning The 3-Legged Race
When Business and Technology Run Together

AS the BTM Institute's first major publication, *Winning The 3-Legged Race - When Business and Technology Run Together*, shows that it is possible to subject business technology to a comprehensive set of management processes and standards. Using the Enamics BTM Framework™ as a foundation, this book proves that this is not just a technology issue. It is, instead, a business issue, one that will not see resolution until enterprises have a fundamentally better way to manage technology's contribution to the value chain.

Through Business Technology Management (BTM), enterprises manage technology in lockstep with the business and create environments in which technology helps *shape* (rather than simply enable) strategic choices. Leading enterprises are working to *synchronize* (rather than simply align) their business and technology decision making. And in the best-managed modern enterprises BTM will ensure that technology ultimately *converges* with the business. This book, therefore, explores what may well be the last opportunity for building and sustaining a competitive edge.

In a three-legged race, the perennial picnic game, two players run with the left leg of one tied to the right leg of the other. Those tied limbs become the "third leg." The teammates who coordinate best are sure winners. That's how executives have to think about managing business technology. If they don't, they run the risk that their competitors will.

Winning The 3-Legged Race examines the interplay of business technology with business strategy, governance, budgeting, organization, risk management, business processes, partnerships, and the marketplace — and offers the theory, real-world examples, and specific advice for executives on running, and winning, the race.

About the Authors

Faisal Hoque

Chairman and CEO, BTM Corporation

Author of *e-Enterprise, The Alignment Effect , Winning The 3-Legged Race, Six Billion Minds* and *Sustained Innovation*

V. Sambamurthy

Eli Broad Professor of IT and Executive Director, Center for Leadership of the Digital Economy, Eli Broad Graduate School of Management, Michigan State University

Co-Chair, BTM Academic Council, BTM Institute

Author of *Unleashing IT-Enabled Value Nets* (Society for Information Management, 2004)

Robert Zmud

Michael F. Price Chair in MIS, University of Oklahoma Michael F. Price College of Business

Co-Chair, BTM Academic Council, BTM Institute

Author of *Framing the Domains of IT Management* (Pinnaflex Educational Resources, 2000)

Tom Trainer

Senior Vice President and Global CIO PepsiCo, Inc.

Co-Chair, BTM Industry Council, BTM Institute

Carl Wilson

Executive Vice President and CIO Marriott International, Inc.

Co-Chair, BTM Industry Council, BTM Institute

For information on this book please visit:
www.btminstitute.org/winningthe3leggedrace/

Six Billion Minds
Managing Outsourcing in the Global Knowledge Economy

THIS publication of the BTM Institute — *Six Billion Minds: Managing Outsourcing in the Global Knowledge Economy* — is a wake-up call to global leaders. A collaboration among the most accomplished academics and global leaders (over 60 top international figures), this book examines management challenges and innovation opportunities in light of the profound impact of globalization and the emergence of the knowledge economy. It shows how to build excellence by leveraging the vast global knowledge pool of the "six billion minds" that make up the emerging knowledge economy, which is driven by the convergence of business and technology.

Globalization is leaving a lasting impression. While not perfect, globalization has been extremely successful for the world economy. It has created millions of jobs, raised millions out of poverty and improved the quality of life in countries that once were considered incapable of contributing to the world economy. Instead of debating its merits, we could better spend our time learning how to thrive in it, rather than letting ourselves get trampled by it. It is the role of *Six Billion Minds* to be a "field guide to globalization."

What is new today is summed up in the term "knowledge economy." We believe that Global Outsourcing = Knowledge Economy. And this economy is about discovering and harnessing the knowledge that can spring forth from any mind, anywhere. *Six Billion Minds* examines the seismic shifts that threaten to engulf long-dominant nations like the United States, whose world leadership in innovation is now being rivaled.

This book tackles the subject with great insights and blunt realities from the business leaders pioneering and setting the pace of global outsourcing as the next big element of the knowledge economy. This economy is about innovation and global outsourcing competitiveness. And sustainable innovation requires a seamless, structured management approach that begins with board and CEO-level issues and connects all the way through technology investment and implementation.

The authors have interviewed the most accomplished business leaders in the world and included not only methods, processes, and practical tips, but also human stories of success and survival — creating this unique exploration of the global knowledge economy.

For information on this book please visit:
www.btminstitute.org/sixbillionminds/

" As the world becomes ever more connected, business leaders will need to recognize the issues set forth in Six Billion Minds. *How to think about these issues, and how to make the right decisions regarding them, is the mission of this book.*"

— *Krishna Palepu*
Ross Graham Walker Professor of Business Administration
Senior Associate Dean, International Development
Harvard Business School

About the Authors

Mark Minevich
Board of Advisors, BTM Institute
Recipient of the Albert Einstein Award
Author of *The CTO Handbook*

Dr. Frank-Jürgen Richter
President, Horasis, The Global Visions Community
Former Director, World Economic Forum, Asian Affairs
Member, BTM Institute
Author of *Global Future, Asia's New Crisis and Recreating Asia*

Faisal Hoque
Chairman and CEO, BTM Corporation
Author of *e-Enterprise, The Alignment Effect, Winning The 3-Legged Race, Six Billion Minds* and *Sustained Innovation*

BTM Research And Education

BTm Institute

In 2003, the Business Technology Management Corporation (BTM Corporation) launched the Business Technology Management Institute (BTM Institute). The international, nonprofit BTM Institute is the first organization of its kind to bring together a select group from the academic, corporate, government and thought leadership communities as a think tank to address the long-standing need to manage business and technology together. The Institute established an academic research agenda, produced major publications, and has begun a much needed and first ever collaboration among multi-disciplinary experts and academics. Today, the BTM Institute is the world's largest and most influential knowledge-based community solely focused on business technology management, with global support from leading academics at Michigan State, University of Oklahoma, Harvard, Emory University, MIT, and the London School of Economics; executives from Coca-Cola, General Motors, Shell Oil, Philip Morris, HBO, PepsiCo Inc., Eli Lilly, Bayer, IBM, Amtrak, United States GSA, Viacom, Xerox and Marriott; former officials from the European Parliament, U.S. Senate, World Bank, and The United Nations; and prominent international figures. The goal of BTM is to lead the industry in 'Making Business and Technology One,' and the BTM Institute is the knowledge network that allows the next generation of leaders to learn from each other.

For more information on the BTM Institute, please visit
www.btmcorporation.research.btminstitute.org

The BTM Academy - Executive Development Programs at BROAD for Business Technology Management is a collaboration between Michigan State University and BTM Corporation to offer executive development programs for business technology management. The goal of these executive development programs is to provide today's leaders with cutting-edge management techniques that address the management challenges, which often result from business model innovation, by converging business and technology. BTM Academy's curriculum leads the industry in making business and technology one in a highly interactive learning environment with a renowned academic faculty, Fortune 100 executives, and industry thought-leaders. Participants in these programs will Discover, Learn, and Collaborate to acquire the expertise required to effectively lead at the enterprise level, and upon completion receive a Business Technology Management (BTM) Certificate of Achievement from the Eli Broad Graduate School of Management.

For more information on the BTM Academy, please visit
www.btmcorporation.research.btmacademy.com

BTM Exchange is a membership based peer-to-peer knowledge community created by the Business Technology Management Corporation (BTM Corporation) to exclusively focus on managing the convergence of business and technology. It offers its members invaluable management insight through non-competing peer-to-peer research, events, discussion forums, and publications on a variety of issues relating to business technology leadership, strategic decision-making, best practices, and relevant career choices through a variety of threaded knowledge exchanges. These knowledge exchanges are delivered through research sessions, hosted dialogues and meetings via a secure online repository and facilitated by world-renowned researchers, thought leaders and industry experts. Through primary research focused around three knowledge tracks: Emerging Models, Key Capabilities, and Operational Excellence, the BTM Exchange peer-to-peer knowledge community collaborates with leading practitioners and researchers to drive management best practices forward. These Exchanges are structured and measured around the BTM Framework™ and the BTM Maturity Model™ that define organization, process, information, and technology to enable key management capabilities.

For more information on the BTM Exchange, please visit
btmcorporation.research.btmexchange.com

Founded in 1999, the Business Technology Management Corporation (BTM Corporation), provides research, products, and management services to bring business and technology together at leading global corporations, governments, and not-for-profit organizations. The company focuses on creating solutions with management processes, software applications, and domain expertise that allow its customers to use technology strategically to build better businesses.

Today, customers such as JPMorgan, Marriott, PACCAR, PepsiCo, Sabre, BNP Paribas, and the French Social Security Agency use BTM Solutions. The wingspan of BTM Corporation's success now exceeds 12 major industries, including manufacturing, consumer goods, hospitality, financial services, insurance, defense, government agencies, and utilities. The company's dedicated R&D process for Business Technology Management (BTM) resulted not only in the creation of the management science of BTM, but also in an unparalleled collection of products/IP and a global knowledge network that ensure our competitive advantage.

Increasingly, through our partners and the BTM Institute, the BTM Academy, and the BTM Press, the BTM Corporation is expanding into the world's largest and most influential knowledge-based community with a sole focus on business technology management. Today global supporters of BTM include leading academics from Michigan State, University of Oklahoma, Harvard, Emory University, MIT, and the London School of Economics; executives from Coca-Cola, General Motors, Shell Oil, Philip Morris, HBO, PepsiCo Inc., Eli Lilly, Bayer, IBM, Amtrak, United States GSA, Viacom, Xerox and Marriott; and former officials from the European Parliament, U.S. Senate, World Bank, and The United Nations among others.

For more information on the BTM Corporation, please visit
www.btmcorporation.com